LINCOLN CHRISTIAN COLLEGE AND SEMINARY

ILLUSTRATED GUIDE TO

DREAMS

Above: Reality is but a merry-go-round.

Right: Angel injecting life.

Far right: The window on the soul.

ILLUSTRATED GUIDE TO
DREAMS

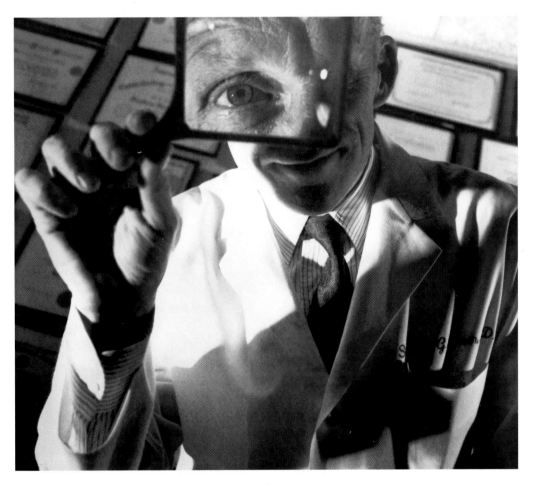

VALERIE FRANCIS

SMITHMARK

Left: The Stairway to Heaven, Jacob's Dream.

Below: Beyond normal horizons, a view of the unconscious.

Bottom: Journey through life.

Copyright © 1995 Brompton Books Corp.

All rights reserved. No part of this publication may be reproduced, stored in a retrieval system or transmitted in any form by any means, electronic, mechanical, photocopying or otherwise, without first obtaining the written permission of the copyright owner.

This edition published in 1995 by Smithmark Publishers a division of U.S. Media Holdings, Inc.
16 East 32nd Street
New York,
New York 10016.

SMITHMARK books are available for bulk purchase for sales promotion and premium use. For details write or telephone the Manager of Special Sales,
SMITHMARK Publishers Inc.,
16 East 32nd Street,
New York, NY 10016.
(212) 532-6600.

Produced by Brompton Books Corp.
15 Sherwood Place,
Greenwich, CT 06830.

ISBN 0-8317-1021-7

Printed in Spain

10 9 8 7 6 5 4 3 2 1

CONTENTS

Gratis

117504

Chapter One

THE HISTORY OF DREAMS

What is the purpose of dreams? Many people believe that they never dream, or that their dreams are simply stuff and nonsense. Everyone is entitled to their own opinion but, by either ignoring or misunderstanding the dream world, we actually throw away amazing opportunities for improving our lives. History proves this to us, but so often belief in the power of dreams is dismissed as the credulity of naive people living without the benefits of our computerized, modern world.

George du Maurier in *Peter Ibbetson* put the former view succinctly: "the whole cosmos is in a man's brains. . . . And when sleep relaxes the will, and there are no earthly surroundings to distract attention . . . the riderless fancy takes the bit in his teeth, and the whole cosmos goes mad and has its wild will of us." He went on to say, "No wonder early man was, in his ignorance, persuaded they conveyed messages to him in which the more clever men of the group saw an opening for personal ascendancy by devising a system of interpretation giving them great importance and leadership in the tribe." Dreams and their interpretations have been recorded since time immemorial and paying attention to them has changed the course of human endeavor. Many great discoveries are the result of dreams: Archimedes, Edison and Einstein, are just three distinguished scientists whose theories developed from dreams.

The writer Joseph Campbell believed that "men were dreaming when they were little more than apes." In *The Heart of the Hunter*, Laurens van der Post quotes a French anthropologist who said: "the dream is the true God of primitive man." It is interesting that records of many early civilizations mention the importance of dreams.

In the Hindu scriptures, the *Upanishads*, dating from between 800 and 400 BC, when questioned by

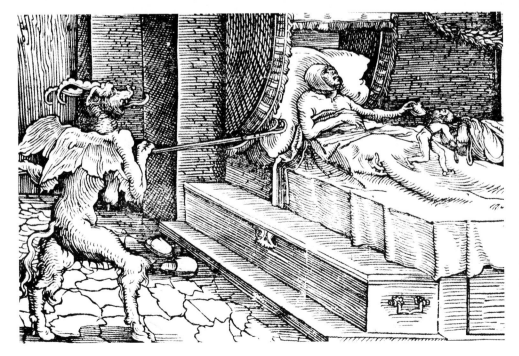

Opposite: The Creation of Eve – God brought her into being while Adam slept.

Left: Sick woman dreaming that she is being taunted by the devil.

"Abandoning of the body ... the Spirit wandering above and below."

the King of Videha, Yajnavalkya said: "Abandoning his body at the gate of dreams the Spirit beholds, in awaking, his senses sleeping. . . . in the region of dreams, wandering above and below the Spirit makes for himself innumerable subtle creations." Similarly the Chinese sage Chuang-tzu wrote: "Once upon a time I, Chuang-tzu, dreamed I was a butterfly. I was conscious only of following my fancies as a butterfly and was unaware of my individuality as a butterfly. Suddenly I was awakened and there I lay myself again. Now I do not know whether I was a man dreaming I was a butterfly or whether I am a butterfly now dreaming I am a man." This identification with being awake has troubled many great thinkers down the ages.

The Sumerians, together with the Assyrians and the Babylonians, all recognized An Za Qar, their god of dreams. The dream of Gilgamesh, King of Sumeria, is one of the most famous, recorded on tablets dating from around 650 BC. He was regularly troubled by dreams which his mother, the goddess Ninsun, interpreted for him. Gilgamesh is warned in a dream of his friend, Enkidu's, death.

Another very early dream is that of the Egyptian king, Thotmes IV *c*. 1420 BC. It is recorded on a sheet of granite between the paws of the Great Sphinx. At that time the Sphinx was neglected and beginning to disappear under the sand. Thotmes dreamt that he would be ruler of Egypt and have a long and prosperous reign. On awakening he saw the Great Sphinx in its sorry state and vowed to keep it beautiful for the rest of his life. The Egyptians were great believers in the power of dreams and oracles. They thought that through dreams they could contact divine sources, receive precognitive messages and also effect healing. They had dream temples where priests and priestesses took the major questions of the day and incubated (seeded) them into the dream state of visionaries, rather like the Greek Delphic Oracle, except that in this instance the answers came from dreams rather than trances or altered states of consciousness. Records show that healing was effected in these dream temples the same way, the cure or the request for a cure, being seeded into the dream. Those who were sick would also sleep in the temples, believing that they would be visited by the god of healing, Imhotep (known as Asclepius to the Greeks and Romans). Priests would then assist with interpretation. A dream example of this is given in Chapter Four. Many hieroglyphics have been discovered on dream interpretation.

Right: Asclepius, the god of healing, Imhotep to the Egyptians, who created the dream temples.

Similar healing temples were to be found in China, where meditating supplicants would dream of visions of the goddess Kwan Yin. In Buddhist and Shinto temples in Japan, where healing was practiced, there were dream oracles. Certain rituals had to be performed to purify the sick petitioner to a state where he could receive guidance and a vision of the ruling deity. The most famous Shinto shrine is at Usa in Kyushi, dedicated to the god, Hachiman.

Islam also practiced a form of incubated dream healing. A very special prayer was said just before sleeping, known as the "istigara." Special prayers were also practised by the Syrians.

The Greeks and Romans were greatly influenced by dreams, and continued to use healing temples. By the fourth century BC there were over 400 dedicated to the god Asclepius, the most famous being at Epidaurus. Their linking feature was Asclepius's symbol, the serpent; in some cases the sick would sleep among snakes to help effect a cure. The symbol of Asclepius, now known as the "caduceus," is still seen today in the badges of many healing professions.

Hippocrates however, believed that dreams were not messages of divine import, but simply diagnostic. Aristotle supported this opinion, considering that they were the result of over-active senses. Plato believed that the liver was the seat of dreams and in a discussion in *The Republic*, Socrates comments that dreams reveal the "violence and lawlessness in us all." Aristotle followed

Left: Dreams played an important part in the lives of the Egyptians.

Right above: The god, Vishnu, sleeping on the serpent, Ananta-Sesha, floating on the Cosmic Ocean. Creation is like a dream within him awaiting manifestation in words.

Right below: Gilgamesh holding the jar of Eternal Life. Through his mother's dream interpretations, Gilgamesh ruled Sumeria.

ed by succeeding generations as the path to salvation. Pharaoh's prophetic dream in the book of Genesis is also well known. Imprisoned by Pharaoh, Joseph interprets a fellow-inmate's dream in prison on the condition that on his release, the prisoner pleads for Joseph's freedom. Two years later, Pharaoh summons Joseph to interpret a particularly troublesome dream, and guided by God, Joseph predicts seven years of plenty, followed by seven years of famine for Egypt. Pharaoh acted on his dream and stored up grain for the lean years. As a result of his advice Pharaoh's power increased and Joseph became one of Pharaoh's trusted advisors.

Moses also knew dreams to be immensely important following guidance from God: "Hear now my words. If there be a prophet among you I, the Lord, will make myself known to him in a vision and will speak to him in a dream." God also appeared to Solomon in a dream which appeared to be lucid, since Solomon participated, asking and receiving answers to his questions.

Another famous Biblical dream was that of Nebuchadnezzar, re-dreamed and interpreted by Daniel. This seems to be the only documented case of someone re-dreaming someone else's dream. It is quite possible to go back into one's own dreams, though. One feels, too, that the interpretation that Daniel gave was somewhat contrived to enable him to say things to the tyrant king that would not normally be permitted, a feat that has been exploited by many wise men and seers down the years.

In the New Testament the most well known dream is in Matthew's gospel, when the angel appeared to Joseph to tell him that Mary was

Hippocrates view that if dreams were messages from the gods, only intelligent men would dream! This attitude survived well into the Middle Ages. Early Christian writers such as Iamblichus (330 AD), differentiated between human dreams and divine visions, and Tertullian (c. 160-230 AD), wrote almost plaintively, "Is it not well known to all people that the dream is the most usual way that God reveals himself to man?" The works of Virgil and Homer are littered with dreams and it is from Virgil that we get the superstition that dreams before midnight are false dreams and those after are the real ones. One of the most compre-

hensive dream books of the ancient world, with theories that are still followed today, is the *Oneirokritika* written by the Roman, Artemidorus of Ephesus.

One of the greatest sources of information on dreams and their effect on the human race is the Bible. All the way through the Old Testament, from the very earliest times, prophetic dreams influenced the path of history. Jacob's magical dream in the book of Genesis about the stairway to heaven lined with angels is well known. Ladders have quite an importance in dream symbology, since, like bridges, they form links and Jacob's ladder was regard-

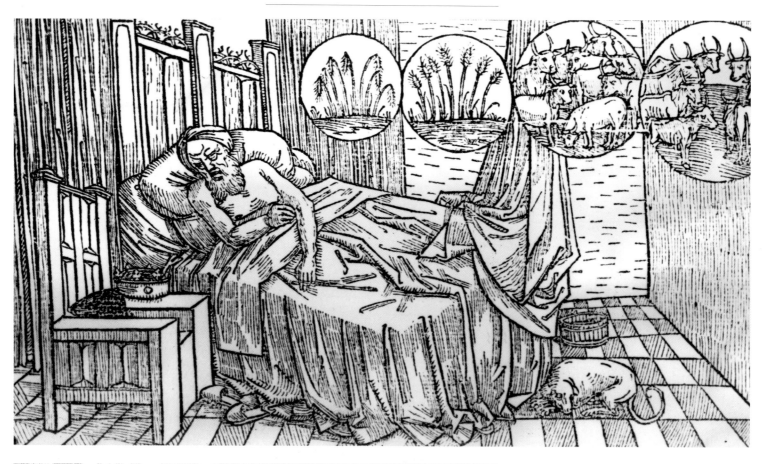

Above: The strange dream of Pharaoh about the seven lean and the seven rich years.

Left: Daniel interpreting the dream of Nebuchadnezzar.

pregnant with a special child. Later, Joseph was advised in another dream to flee to Egypt when Herod wanted to kill the Messiah, and in a final dream was told he could return safely to Israel after Herod's death. The dream that was ignored was that of Pilate's wife telling him to have nothing to do with Jesus. Who knows what may have happened if Pilate had acted differently? All these dreams are clearly reported in the book of Matthew.

The Talmud, the ancient Rabbinic writings, also mentions dreams in the Babylonian version. Hesda said, "A dream not interpreted is like a letter not read." Research also shows that in the works of Alkindi in Arabia the system used for dream interpretation was highly sophisticated.

Many medieval scholars and mystics were interested in dreams. The fourth-century saint, Gregory of Nyssa, known as the "Illuminator," and who eventually became patriarch of Armenia, did much research into dreams. He followed the views of Aristotle but also clearly defined the difference between god-sent visions and regular dreams. The latter, he felt, were truly related to the human condition expressing senses, emotions, and passions, a revolutionary idea at the time. Moving through history, many strange opinions emerge, some valid and others

Thomas Aquinas was the first person to discuss the synchronicity of dreams and events.

Left: St. Francis of Assisi experienced many powerful dreams which he acted on.

completely odd. St. Hildegard of Bingen, a tenth-century nun, experienced visions from an early age, and was interested in the difference between them and her dreams. The latter she categorized as either prophecy or simply mundane, but warned people to beware of demons masquerading as divine beings. Michael Scott (*c.* 1175-1230), a Scottish scholar known as the "wondrous wizard," translated the works of Aristotle and other classical writers. He specialized in astrology and was the first to add date, time and place of birth, together with the position of the planets to dream interpretation.

The thirteenth-century theologian Thomas Aquinas and the Franciscan scholar, Bartholomeo Angelicus, both felt that it was important not to put too much store in the meanings of dreams, or to mistake them for divine visions. Aquinas, however, felt that there was "a single cause of both the dream and the event," which we know today as synchronicity from the work of Jung. St. Francis of Assisi experienced powerful dreams, one of the most significant being one about a tall tree. As he gazed at it, he became the same size and easily bent and twisted it. At the same time the pope dreamed that the basilica of the Lateran had been prevented from falling by someone of extreme insignificance. The work of St. Francis was highly-valued; in an

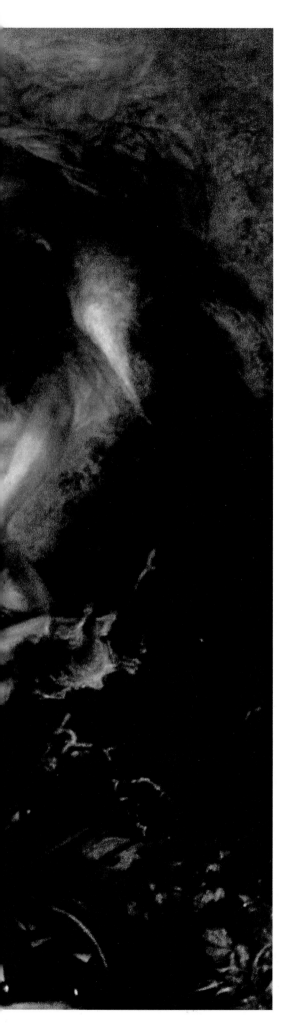

Left: Joseph's dream of the sun, moon and eleven stars making obeisance to him.

Above: God created Eve while Adam looks on.

age when church corruption was widespread, his honesty and purity inspired people, and as suggested by both these dreams, strengthened the Catholic church.

The early Celtic stories from the Welsh, Irish and Scottish oral legends are saturated with dreams. They are very much about the "matter of Britain" and precede the Arthurian tales which were recorded by Geoffrey of Monmouth in the twelfth century.

Many of the more powerful of the recorded Celtic dreams are about the feminine aspect in her triple form which, in the Celtic belief system, was interpreted as the land (the earth mother) and came to represent the sovereignty of Britain. The *aisling* of the Irish is the archetypal female who leads the hero to the underworld, where he drinks of the cup of wisdom to prepare himself for kingship.

A dream of significance to the historical pattern of Britain, the Dream of Macsen Wledig, is found in the Welsh collection of tales, the *Mabinogion*. The Emperor of Rome, Macsen Wledig, had a dream that from a high mountain top he could

see a lovely island. He made his way to it and found a castle. On entering, he saw two young men playing *gwyddbwyll* (a form of chess, symbolically representing the land of Britain), watched by a beautiful golden-haired maiden, who allowed him to embrace her. At that point the canopy collapsed and Macsen was rudely awakened. He was so taken with his dream maiden that he determined to find her. He sent out a messenger who discovered her and led him eventually to Britain where he found everything as in his dream. Thus the maiden Elen, representing the sovereignty of Britain, became Princess of Rome and she and her brother were given lands in Brittany.

Many may be familiar with the legend of the princesses who turned into swans, the Daughters of Llyr. In this Irish tale, the dream of Oengus tells how he repeatedly dreamt of a beautiful maiden who vanished just as he went to kiss her. The endless frustration made him ill and eventually a search was made. She was found near a lake with other girls who were all changed into swans once a year. Oengus released her from her swan form and brought her

home. And there are many more beautiful dreams, showing how the legendary history of the land depended on the correct interpretation of dreams to preserve sovereignty.

It is really to Sigmund Freud that we owe our current interest in dreams. He believed that dreams could not be ignored in the understanding of the personality. He felt that dreams revealed a part of us that could not be easily accessed in any other way. He thought that the personality had three distinct parts: the ego, the lower unconscious, which needed instruction from the id, the conscious, which contained all the drives, and the superego or higher mind, which is the psychic level. This theory is very similar to that held by the Polynesian people. The id was seen as the mediator between the ego and the superego.

Freud regarded the desire for life as our prime motivation and, believed that humans are driven by their procreative instincts, that is sex. He also considered the possibility of death instincts as well, but did not elaborate on this. He felt that many restraints on behavior appeared in childhood through our guilt and conflict with authority and many infantile wishes are therefore repressed. He suggested that during sleep our censor had less energy and allowed repressed desires out of the bag via the wish fulfilment dream.

To explore this, Freud encouraged patients to talk about their dreams and any thoughts that they provoked, a process later known as the "free association of ideas," which produced marked results. However, with his rigid views he fell victim to the "experimenter effect," a danger for all dream interpreters, and tried to impose his dogma on others, seeing only what he wanted to see.

In the early part of his career Carl Gustav Jung worked with Freud, but there came a point when their views

Left: Early stories from the Welsh, Irish and Scottish oral legends are saturated with dreams.

Sigmund Freud, the father of modern ideas of interpretation.

diverged and gradually their association died. Jung developed the idea of the ego beyond simple repressed sex and wish fulfilment. He considered it to be a well of personal information which was fed from an even greater source, the "collective unconscious." He theorized that not only did dreams provide a key to our current problems, but that also they advised us how to develop our full human potential. What was important, however, was to interpret the dream with all its many various and symbolic meanings before applying it to the dreamer's situation, which could incorrectly color the result. In

Jung's words, constantly ask "What is the dream saying?"

When considering techniques, Jung had a relativistic opinion and constantly asserted that "the wrong technique in the hands of the right person will achieve the desired result; the right technique in the hands of the wrong person will fail." This is particularly important today, when problems such as false memory syndrome are raising their ugly heads. The analyst needs to be constantly on guard. Jung also used free association, but did not allow his clients to wander too far.

It was Jung who described us as

living in a beautiful house, the mansion of the soul, but rarely leaving the basement. With this idea he was able to apply the imagery to the human situation.

He developed the masculine and feminine aspects, the animus and anima respectively, as being present within the human psyche. He considered they should be well-balanced but that frequently there was an over-dominance in one direction or the other to the detriment of normal functioning for the individual. Alongside these he added the ego and its shadow.

Jung was the first to formulate the psychological concept of archetypes as a unique principle from a primordial source. They are images that emerge from the level of the collective unconscious, things and symbols that we react to without conscious thought. He created a list of 12 major personalities with their shadow sides which could materialize in the dream state. Again, these are covered later in the book.

Edgar Cayce (1877-1945), known as the "Sleeping Prophet," had much to say on dreams. While in an altered state of consciousness, similar to the dream state, he was able to help people in many ways. His work, known as "readings," consisted of transcripts of his trance communications. People came to him with problems, physical, mental or spiritual and often received profound and thought-provoking answers. He was able to diagnose and heal while in this state and it was not necessary for the patient to be with him or even in the same house – distance was irrelevant. He also came out with entire discourses on subjects such as meditation.

He felt dreams to be our sixth

Right: Carl Gustav Jung, a contemporary of Freud, who developed the theory of archetypes and synchronicity.

Left: Edgar Cayce, the "sleeping prophet" who in the dream state healed and produced many profound prophesies.

sense, that we tuned into higher levels in dreams and became aware of what is being built and what may be projected into the physical in the future. In fact our whole future is built in this way. This can give credence to pre cognitive dreams.

He was another advocate of working with dreams rather than interpreting them. "Whatever they may be, our dreams are what they should be. Therefore, we may truly say there are no bad dreams, because the dream is an objective report on the complex combination of forces which are operative in our life at the time." (Pruyear, *The Edgar Cayce Primer.*)

Chapter Two

OTHER CULTURES

I t is important to realize that dreaming can mean different things to people in different cultures and it is, therefore, useful to have some idea of the ethnic background of the dreamer before pontificating on possible meanings. Western culture often dismisses dreaming as superficial nonsense, but many other cultures actually pay profound attention to dreams and act on the advice given.

Australian aboriginal tradition has it that the whole of life appears to be enacted in the "dreamtime" or *altjeringa*, *tjukurapa* or the *Bamun*, according to tribal origins. To quote A.W. Reed's book, *Aboriginal Tales*, "In the Dream world, man dreamed splendid dreams of kinship with everything that surrounded him and invented glorious tales, as well as horrific ones, to provide a satisfying account of the origin of natural life with which he was so familiar, investing what most of us accept as commonplace with the supernatural." The aboriginal creation myth equates all time as existing simultaneously. There is no past, present or future. It is all in the now. They live in a magical place of the permanent no-where, no-when of the myth and they consider themselves at all times to be dreaming the dream.

Left: Many weird effigies were created shaped in surrealistic dreamlike images.

Right: The Australian aborigines consider themselves at all times to be dreaming the dream.

Many of their tribes are totally dependent on what dreams foretell. They posses such a vivid imagination and inward intensity that at times it is impossible to differentiate between the waking and dreaming state.

An example of their beliefs is their

ability to traverse vast inhospitable country. Members of the tribe dream their totem animal, say a kangaroo, and then manifest it in surrounding terrain, either as an actual animal or an outline in trees, rock formations or other natural phenomena. These then act as perfectly reliable signposts.

A similar viewpoint is expressed by the bushmen of the Kalahari. In *The Heart of the Hunter*, Laurens van der Post, tells of how when pressed to explain their creation myths as a comparison with those of the Christian, the Bushman said: "But you see, it is very difficult, for always there is a dream dreaming us." Van der Post goes on to say that "Believing as I do that the dream is not a waste product of the mind expelled through some sewage system of the spirit, but a manifestation of the first and abiding meaning, I thought I should enlarge St. John's theme to include the idea that in the beginning there was a dream. This dream was with God and indeed was God. Somehow this dream demanded that it should be lived. As St. John

The mysterious Ayers rock, where many aboriginal paintings have been found.

might have put it, 'the dream was made flesh.' "

Other African societies set great store by dreams, believing that their destiny is involved. They have a deep belief in ancestor worship, that wisdom can be accessed through making contact with the spirits of the past. Dreams are a natural source for such communications. They are convinced that their ancestors care about their lives and through dreams will inform them of important future events, pleasures or disasters, which naturally enables sensible preparations to be made. Records show successful cures for sickness from dream messages and even political decisions are made from time to time based on dream advice. It can, of course, be a two edged sword, with negative actions resulting. Sometimes they are convinced that nightmares are actually sent to them, that through dreams people can wish

The shamanistic medicine men use dream techniques for healing.

evil on them or even death.

Dr. Roderick Peters, a medical doctor who practiced in West Africa, states that patients frequently described their dreams when they came to consult him. It was apparent that they felt there to be a distinct relevance between the dream state and their illnesses. It was fairly commonplace for the local witch doctors to put spells on people, which patients thought the Western doctor could remove. However, Dr. Peters quotes a case where he could do nothing and a perfectly healthy individual died within eight days with no symptoms whatsoever of physical disease.

In the philosophy of the Polynesian islands, known as *Huna*, the psyche is divided into three distinct parts – the low self, *unihipili*; the middle self, *uhane*, and the high self or *aumakua*. Their theory is that the low self is the unconscious, instinctual side of the personality which holds the memory banks. The middle self is the conscious and log-

ical part, while the high self is the wise and spiritual part. The middle self cannot communicate directly with the high self so to get things to happen, the middle self needs to instruct the low self.

They believe that in the dream state the high self of *aumakua* is on guard and implants ideas to the low self. These can be in the form of advice, warnings or information of the future. To quote Dr. Erika Nau, "In sleep the high self collects the thoughts projected by the low and middle selves and fashions the blueprint for the individual's future. When the sleeper has put himself into jeopardy with his thinking, the high self steps in and warns of the consequences. These warnings may be accepted or rejected, for we have free will." This is a different concept from the usual divine guidance theory.

There is an interesting incident recorded by Arthur Grimble in his book *A Pattern of Islands* based on his time in the Pacific Islands. He recalls a feverish pregnant woman

Medicine man from the Southern Highlands of Papua New Guinea.

whose sleep was restless and fraught with nightmares. One of the villagers, Obadaia, sat and hummed to her for hours on end. On awakening from a long period of quiet sleep she said "It was queer. I kept on having nightmares . . . then I remember thinking I was wide awake and hearing a quiet humming sound all round me. Everything seemed marvellous. I suppose it was a dream, too, but I didn't have another after that. I still feel wonderful, as if nothing could possibly go wrong." Obadaia knew that his humming would work and would not leave her until she settled. This again shows an instinctual knowledge of how to communicate with the low self to control the dream world and induce peaceful sleep.

One of the most well-known exponents of dreaming is extolled by Carlos Castenada in his series of books about the Yaqui Indian sorcerer, Don Juan Matus. To understand him, one needs a certain belief in parallel universes, which we can learn to inhabit at will. It is simply a matter of conditioning and understanding of altered states of consciousness. Don Juan called this the art of dreaming or the "gateway to infinity." He felt it to be a two stage exercise combining how to do it with what it means when you achieve it.

Castenada gave over many years of his life to working on these techniques, and quotes Don Juan in a clear statement of the dream: "Dreaming, can only be experienced. Dreaming is not just having dreams; neither is it daydreaming or wishing or imagining. Through dreaming we can perceive other worlds, which we can certainly describe, but we can't describe what makes us perceive them. Yet we can feel how dreaming opens up those other realms. Dreaming seems to be a sensation – a process in our bodies, an awareness in our minds." Don Juan saw dreams as aids to develop mental and psychic powers. He advocated lucid dreaming to enable the dreamer to manipulate the results. One had to be conscious to achieve real benefit. A study of Castenada's books and the practice of the propounded ideas will truly lead to other ways of living.

In the Tibetan *Book of the Dead* dreaming is mentioned as the intermediate stage between life and death and that it is a form of preparation for the eventual transition. When we fall asleep "we find ourselves in a dream-world similar to the *bardo* of becoming. Here we take on a dream body and go through dream experiences . . . all of which we believe to be solid and real, without ever realizing that we are dreaming." Dreams were important to these high mountain people who felt them to be vital for their spiritual growth. If the dream seemed particularly significant or worrying they would visit the priest at the local monastery for interpretations. In Tibetan medicine out-of-body states are always examined as being of significance. Denise Linn quotes a Tibetan method of dream recall where you imagine a glowing blue sphere in the throat area in which you place your desire for recall and hold the image until falling asleep. She goes on to say that research has shown that the back of the throat controls dream activity.

The Senoi people of Malaysia are frequently quoted in dream literature because they lived their lives through the perspective of dreams. Each day dreams were shared either in the family or within the group. Interpretation was a joint enterprise and solutions offered for difficult dreams with appropriate actions being taken to improve the dreamer's life and attitudes. Good dreams were praised and precognitive ones acknowledged with the correct preparation for them to occur. Lucid dreaming was encouraged and general rules applied. Dangers in dreams had to be confronted, pleasure on whatever level participated in, and a clear ending needed to be achieved to each dream. Death was to do with the end of things and should, therefore, be experienced in the dream. Sex and dream lovers should be acknowledged and enjoyed in all their facets. Often help was provided by dream guides. As a result of these practices, the psychological attitudes of these people were well balanced.

Most of the Native American tribes believed implicitly in dreaming, to the extent that they set aside particular nights specifically for dreaming because they considered that the survival of the tribe as well as the individual could depend on it. Like the other cultures, they felt it difficult to define the border between the waking and dream state. Lucid dreaming was common and incubation the norm to assist with healing, hunting and fertility. They were also known to amplify

A Tibetan priest in Katmandu.

dreams to bring about healing. An example of such appears in Vogel's *American Indian Medicine:* "In 1676 in the Onondaga country, we are told that the medicine men persuaded the parents of a sick girl that she had seen nine feasts in dreams, and that if they gave these feasts she would be cured." Dream guides were common, either in human form or as power animals. (Could this account for the regular appearance of Native Americans as guides in the Western tradition?) They were treated like friends and counsellors, to be consulted at any time, day or night.

Denise Linn gives very clear accounts of the Native American use of dreams. She tells of how they would travel great distances to act out ritual dream dramas. There was an annual festival called the "Honoraria" where dreams would be acted out theatrically. This was known as the *Ondinnonk.* They felt that this was of crucial importance and that failure to acknowledge the messages of dreams could bring dire results.

Certain tribes believed in the Great Dream which ruled each person's life. They maintained that each

Left: A North American Indian totem pole, a focus of daily meetings.

Below: The dream catcher. The initiate learns to catch the messages of the element of air.

person has one dream which was dreamed in the womb and which was forgotten at birth, which we strive throughout life to remember. All our good characteristics such as courage, creativity, wisdom, consideration of others, etc., were considered to be talents bestowed in this Great Dream. Children are encouraged to remember and explore their dreams from the youngest age, and young men would fast until they had

When a Borneo Dyak dreams of falling in the water he thinks he's lost his spirit and gets a wizard to retrieve it.

visions of their "song of life." Originally, dream catching was part of the initiation ceremonies of certain tribes. The initiate had to learn this art. He made a magical circle around himself and then incubated his visions and dreams. The idea was to capture the messages from the spirits in the element of air enclosed within his circle. The dream catcher is the physical expression of this particular rite.

Dream Lodges are mentioned by Jamie Sams in *Medicine Cards*, where contact is made with power animals (among other things) through whom much of the past wisdom of the tribes is shared. In her book, Lizard is the authority on dreaming. In the medicine story Lizard explains to Snake who wants

to share his shade spot: "Dreaming is going into the future, Snake. I go to where *future* lives. That is why I know you won't eat me today. I dreamed you and I know you're full of mouse.' Lizard is the shadow side of reality where your dreams are reviewed before you decide to manifest them physically."

So many cultures take dreams seriously because they feel that their souls go travelling and they are afraid their souls may get lost. When a Borneo Dyak dreams of falling into the water, he supposes that this accident has befallen his spirit, and he sends for a wizard who fishes for the spirit until he catches it and restores it to its owner. An Indian in Brazil or Guinea believes his dream self has been away hunt-

ing while his body has been sleeping soundly in his hammock. A Macusi Indian, who awoke in ill health, dreamt that his employer had made him haul his canoe up a series of difficult rapids. The following morning he reproached his master for making him toil all night. In Lapland, when a pregnant woman was near her time, she was expected to dream of an ancestor who would tell her which soul from the dead would be born again in her child, and, therefore, what name it should have.

Shamanism was and still is practiced among many cultures in the world, particularly by Native Americans and the cultures of northern Europe, Asia, and the Arctic. It was also practiced by the Celts. The training of the Shaman is deeply involved with altered states of consciousness which frequently contain dreaming. It is usually a difficult and painful route requiring great dedication. The would-be shaman firstly, needs to learn absolute discipline of mind and body. He needs complete control of thought and the power of thought. Then follows the initiation of ritual death and rebirth, which takes place in an altered state. In many cultures it is drug-induced and we find examples of this in Castenada and Wolf. However, it is much more powerful in the dream/meditative state since the brain is not impaired or influenced by external stimulation. The novice learns to make contact with both his and the collective unconscious through a route that he can command at any moment without any assistance.

During this "death" sequence he confronts the shadow side of himself which can manifest as being attacked by wild animals, being tortured and slowly destroyed, a complete dismemberment. It is a complete disintegration of his known personality. All these terrors have to be overcome. He makes contact with his totem animal (familiar) and learns to communicate with others. He learns to shape-shift. A total reconstruction of his psyche takes place. He learns to tune into the infinite wisdom.

In Drury's *The Shaman and the Magician*, Dr. Petri says, "Dreams would reveal to the would-be 'doctor man' that the high god Unggud would 'kill' him. The aborigine would see a giant snake with arms and hands. Then Unggud would take him to a cave and transform him. Unggud gives him a new brain, puts in his body white quartz crystals for secret strength and reveals his future duties. He awakes with a great feeling of inner light.

Instruction, guidance and experience follow for many months, even years."

Having used the dream state for his initiation, the shaman continues to use it for the benefit of those around him. In the case of healing, he uses dream incubation methods similar to those in the ancient dream temples. After elaborate purifying rites the patient seeds his dream with a request for the correct treatment to cure him.

In conjunction with the trance, which can be so extreme as to give the appearance of an epileptic fit, the Shamans also use the dream for their own divinations. In this context it has a similarity to lucid dreaming in that they definitely control the turn of events. They are also able to find appropriate cures, get advice, foretell the future, or shape-shift to overcome negative energies.

An Eskimo shaman outside her tent.

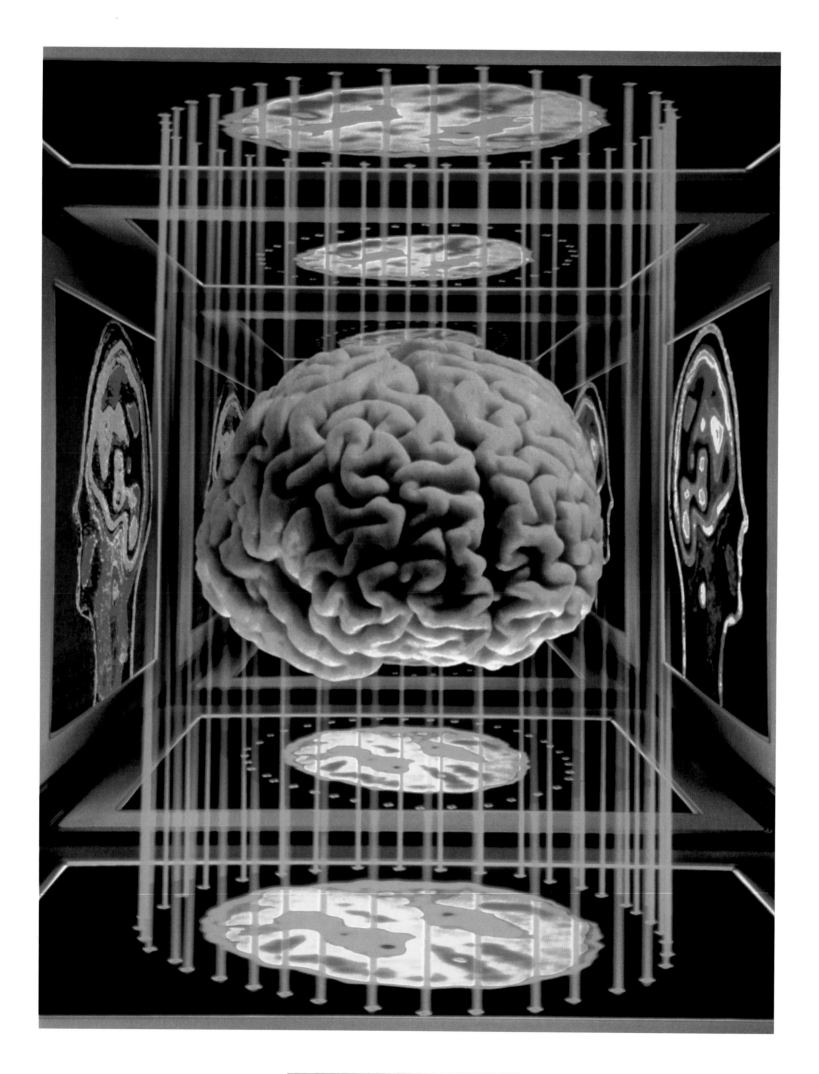

Chapter Three

THE PHYSIOLOGY OF SLEEP

It is important to understand something of the nature of sleep and dreaming on a physiological level. Much exploration has taken place during this century in a laboratory environment to try to discover what actually happens during the one third of our lives we spend asleep. Once we thought that the only reason for sleeping was to rest the body. However, we now know that this is not so and that the brain is more active during sleep. The physical body can be rested without actually sleeping. Now it is thought that we sleep in order to dream.

It has been discovered that there are two main types of sleep, extremely deep sleep is interspersed with periods of lighter sleep combined with rapid eye movements, generally known as REM sleep, (although there are other terms, such as emergent sleep or paradoxical sleep). A great deal of research in Britain has been carried out by Dr Keith Hearne who has invented a dream machine. This machine is sensitive to changes in breathing and skin resistance and is designed to wake the dreamer when

The human brain can now be scanned to reveal its many secrets.

in the REM state.

Most of our dreaming takes place in the REM state when the images are usually specific and non-fuzzy. Those dreams with a shadowy, inconclusive tone are rarer and relate to lower levels of sleep. These stages connect quite distinctly with brain activity and dream scientists have acquired a knowledge of the workings of the brain.

Using EEG (electroencephalogram) machines it has been possible to record the different frequencies of the brainwaves. There are four wave patterns generally acknowledged. The normal waking rhythms are known as Beta waves operating at 15 cycles per second (cps) and faster. This is the period of active thinking and alert attentiveness. They are used during our waking hours and for all major activities. The focus of the brain is external and the brainwave strength is increased by anxiety and reduced by muscular activity. Next are Alpha waves, operating at approximately 7.5 to 15 cps, which equate to relaxed wakefulness. This level is the one where we are relaxing consciously. It is the level of meditation, daydreaming, and hypnosis. At this level flashbacks can occur and physical sensations such

as floating, rocking or swaying. The Theta level, at 4.5 to 7.5 cps, is the area where we are drifting from drowsiness into light sleep. It is the level where hypnogogic images occur and is the main frequency in dreaming itself. Finally, the Delta level, 0.5 to 4.5 cps, is that of deep sleep. Some research shows a connection between Delta and the onset of paranormal phenomena and higher levels of consciousness.

It has been discovered that there is a regular pattern of sleeping. Each occasion begins with a period of deep sleep. (or non-REM sleep – NREM). The sleeper sinks into the slowest level of brain activity for up to 90 minutes. Experiments have shown that this is followed by a short period of REM activity with a further return to deep sleep. This alternation continues throughout the night with the REM periods becoming longer. This pattern has a definite relevance to the feelings on awakening, since if the REM periods are reduced or interrupted the sleeper complains of not having slept well. It is interesting, therefore, to realize that chronic tiredness may well be related to the amount of dreaming that we miss rather than the number of hours of sleep.

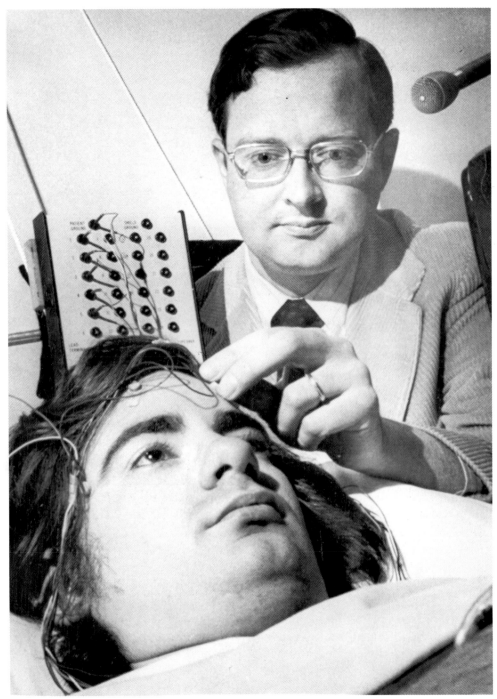

A volunteer being connected to a dream machine to enable him to access his dreams.

One of the problems in modern civilized cultures is the belief in the "eight hours sleep per night" hypothesis, leading to remarkable stress if it is not fulfilled. However, in the main, we should be advised by our bodies, which are completely aware of our needs, be they three hours or ten hours. Once the worry is removed so, frequently, is the sleeplessness. What is important is the quality of that sleep and here current lifestyles tend to interfere.

Deprivation of REM sleep has an extremely marked effect on sub-jects. Exploration under laboratory conditions shows mental and behavioral abnormalities such as aggression, disorientation, difficulty in concentrating, hallucinations and sometimes psychosis. Similar results were discovered under non-laboratory conditions. It has also been noted that the sleeper spends more time in REM sleep following a deprivation period.

Narcolepsy is excessive and uncontrollable attacks of deep sleep, characterized by omission of the NREM stage. These are different from sleeping-in to compensate for a loss of sleep. There almost seems to be a desire on the part of the subject to remain in the sleep state in order to dream. Another feature of this form of sleep is the frequent occurrence of nightmares and anxiety dreams. Frequent spontaneous napping can take place for similar reasons to narcolepsy, i.e. as an escape mechanism. On testing, napping also appears to contain less NREM in the early stages.

There are many theories on what dreams actually are. We know that when we stare hard at something and then close our eyes we have a reverse image on the retina which lasts from some minutes. The same occurs if we look out of a window before closing the eyes. We have a photo negative of a light frame with dark squares or rectangles. We are also aware of shadows and varying light and shade with our eyes completely closed. These are perfectly natural phenomena

It has also been discovered that if we close our eyes and concentrate our attention on one spot as though our eyes were open, we begin to see transient points of light, some coloured moving and colliding. This was researched by Henri Bergson in France around the turn of the century. He theorized that these were caused by blood circulation in the retina and that the mind used them to create dream shapes and images, with the story provided by the imagination.

It is important to understand something of the workings of the body in the sleep state. It is perfectly natural for our metabolism to change. Our eyelids cease blinking, our breathing slows down, whilst the body temperature, blood pressure and heart rate reduce together with the gradual decrease in the cycles of the brainwaves. As we awaken, the process is reversed and all these different phases can be translated in the mind of the sleeper, as part of the dream

Apnea, when the breathing of a sleeper stops for several seconds, is a normal physical condition that is most common in new-born babies, but can appear at any age. It can also occur occasionally in extremely deep meditation as the breath becomes shallower and shallower until it reaches a temporary cessation. It is rarely dangerous.

External noises also have an influence on dreams. How often has the alarm clock been metamorphosized into all manner of monsters, fire engines, sirens, police cars in the dream mind? Any crash or bang in the night gets similar treatment and a snoring partner can be translated as a rumbling earthquake or a snarling animal and as for a screaming vixen, well . . . All these externals need to be examined before arriving at any form of interpretation. "I dreamt my husband was swinging the door too and fro trying to encourage my daughter to enter. I was worried. Then I was near a serving hatch that did not shut properly and a mangy tiger jumped through it to grab some chewed bones near me. I woke thinking I must keep the doors closed. I then heard the radio that had been on for some time giving yet another set of news headlines, one of which was the death of the comedian Larry Grayson whose catch phrase was 'shut that door!' My subconscious hearing the headline repeated had picked it up and made its own interpretation." Some noises are internal rather than actual, and manifest as an explosion or a shot inside the head or occasionally as a brilliant white light. These are physical in origin and are believed to originate from a build-up of static electricity that stimulates the occipital area of the brain.

Sleep paralysis manifests in the dream state as a complete inability, to move in any way or even cry out. During certain levels of sleep the muscular reflexes associated with the limbs and throat disappear and the person is in actuality paralysed. This condition can penetrate the dream state and continue into complete wakefulness, which can be very frightening. Could this paraly-

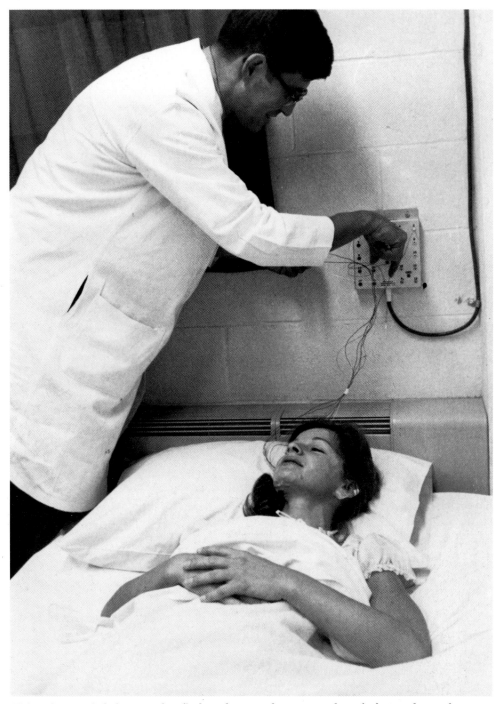

This volunteer is being tested to find out how much we remember of what we hear when we are asleep.

sis be a control to keep us lying down and out of trouble? "My mother used to have a regular nightmare that she was lying in the desert. Something was approaching. She was terrified because she could not move. All her limbs seemed huge and completely unresponsive. Each time it came closer, but it never actually got her."

Catalepsy has a similar sensation except that there is rigidity in the muscles and greater consciousness of the immobile state that creates an equal feeling of helplessness. However, the simple act of opening the eyes seems to bring the body back under conscious control. Catalepsy is often the result of extreme stress combined with incorrect sleeping conditions. A soft bed yields to the shape of the body allowing the tensed muscles to be accommodated, whereas a hard bed encourages the body to relax in order to sleep. "I dreamt that I was swimming in an endless ocean. There was no land in sight any where

and I could feel my strength failing. Gradually, my legs and feet began to stiffen; then my body and finally as I was desperately thrashing with my arms to keep afloat, my arms became rigid too and I knew I was going to sink. Then I woke up, my throat absolutely stiff from trying to shout out."

Another common experience is that of twitching in sleep. Sometimes this becomes a much more pronounced and sudden jolt, the myoclonic jerk, which tends to occur either on falling asleep or on waking. There are two theories on this. Firstly, that it is a sudden contraction of the muscles, and secondly, that it is to do with relaxation of the deeper muscle structure – that sudden spasm as these release when we thought we had already let go completely. Again, the dream mind translates this into the dream, the sensation of stepping off a step that isn't there is quite common, or walking off a precipice. "I am walking up a spiral staircase in a castle. I come to a door and it is very dark. I open the door and walk through. There is an awful sensation as I step into nothing."

Sleep-walking and sleep-talking indicate that the normal relaxation of the muscular reflexes is not taking place. This is usually associated with times of extreme anxiety and stress in daily life. Some schools of thought consider it to be caused by incorrect firing mechanisms in the brain. It can manifest as simple walking round the room or muttering a few words or extremely violent and dangerous action and loud shouting or singing. It is possible to converse with a sleep-talker but often the responses are unintelligible or lack coherence. Unless, of course, they are behaving violently, it is usually unwise to awaken a sleep-walker since they can be excessively disorientated. Far better to lead them safely back to bed. Here is an instance experienced by a friend of mine.

A Japanese device designed to allow one to sleep standing in a crowded place.

"She was sharing a college room with a friend, who frequently sat up late reading whilst Murry fell asleep. On this occasion, Murry sat straight up in bed and announced in a profound voice: 'I have just discovered the secret of the Universe'. 'Tell me.' requested the friend. 'Mind your own business.' was the response. You can imagine the teasing that took place the following day."

An interesting piece of research has shown that not all subjects are in crisis, many are leading well balanced and healthy lives, with the occasional nightmare when life is not going smoothly. In the older generation the physical degeneration can be the result of disease or neurological problems. It is interesting that Helen Keller, who was deaf and blind, actually talked in her sleep before she eventually learned to speak in her waking state.

Snoring is purely physical and can be due to sinus problems, allergies or physically impaired mechanics in the nostril. From time to time it can affect the vocal cords – again, a physical problem rather than part of dreaming. There is, however, another similar sound that is more of a growl that can be related to sleep talking.

Enuresis (or bed-wetting) mainly occurs in disturbed children, usually when there is an excess of authority. Also it can be caused by a weakness in the muscles which allows leaking of the full bladder when the body lets go of its natural muscular reflexes. The full bladder is certainly one physical aspect which inhabits the dream world in many guises. Bruxism (grinding the teeth) tends to have the same roots as enuresis with a contrary reaction of the muscles. It is usually stress related or a sign of deep rooted anger.

Sexual reactions are normal and quite common in the dream state. There are simple physical explanations, whilst at the same time acknowledging that the dream thoughts can produce physical reactions in the same way that waking thoughts do. Laboratory studies

Sometimes the sleeper goes walking.

show that 80% of men have erections in the REM periods. Tests have also shown that paraplegic or quadriplegic, of both sexes, experience orgasm in the dream state. An interesting fact that has come to light in research is that homosexuals have many heterosexual dreams.

Research shows that young babies, who spend most of their time sleeping, have considerable periods of REM and some researchers suggest that dreaming was taking place before birth. This could relate to the

bodily resources being required for the growth process and current research shows secretion of the growth hormone during sleep. The same applies to illness where the natural reaction is to sleep to assist in the repairs. Too often this is interrupted and food is forced. Not only is the body disturbed out of its sleep pattern but it is also obliged to concentrate on digestion rather than the healing process. The immune system also relies for its health on deep sleep. Bacteria in the intestines pro-

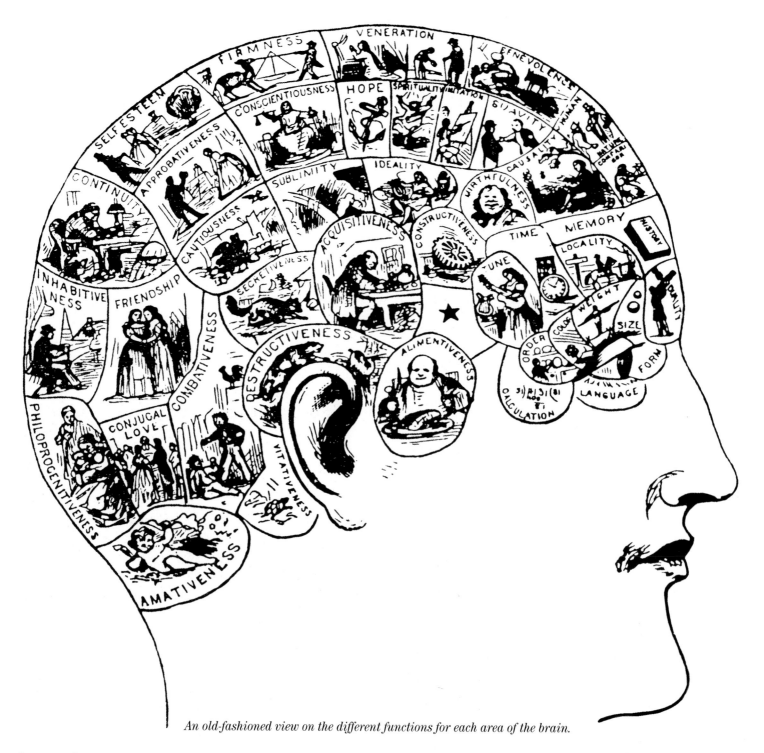

An old-fashioned view on the different functions for each area of the brain.

duce sleep-inducing chemicals which, on reaching the brain set in motion a chain of chemical events to produce defensive cells.

Sleep learning is still controversial. Tests have shown that the NREM period has its value for absorbing on an instinctive level, but that the REM period seems better for taking in new facts. The Alpha state appears to be of more value.

A number of things attributed to sleep disturbance are avoidable. Watching frightening or stimulating television programs, attending lectures, having drastic arguments, or any distressing situation will naturally excite brain activity. Many forms of food and drink have a reputation such as cheese, coffee, spicy food or a large meal. This is entirely a subjective matter with little proven truth except that the stomach obviously needs its rest. Abuse of alcohol is the most common cause of sleep disturbance. This leads to very deep sleep for the first 90 minutes. The following period of REM sleep can hardly

manifest since the surfacing and speeding up of the brainwaves is extremely sluggish. The subject remains mostly in the deep Delta state. The next phase is of extreme wakefulness followed by deep and fitful sleep and an extreme reluctance to wake up in the morning. This means that the normal dream state has not been able to function correctly which could account for

Right: A sleep walker in a "dangerous" position!

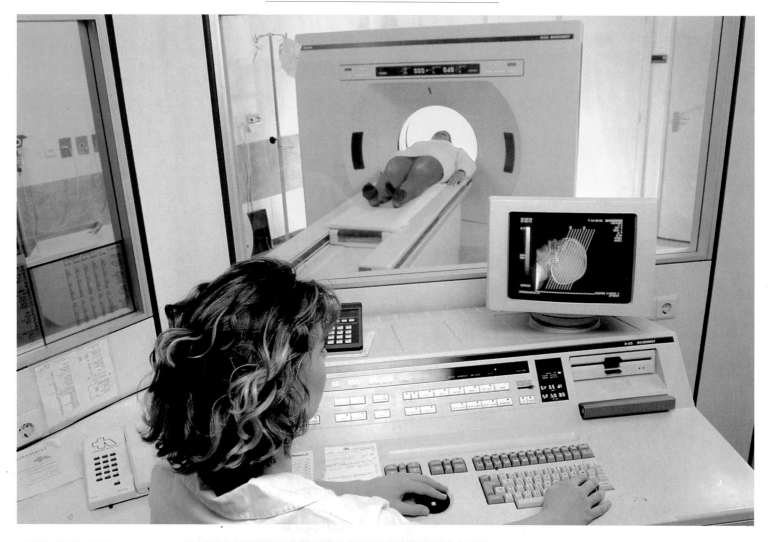

Above: The modern approach to brain function, the CAT scan.

Left: Extra security in the sleep state.

Right: Sexual reactions are quite normal in the dream state.

the symptoms of hangover and/or addiction. Alcoholics also frequently have frightening nightmares often involving ferocious animals or hallucinations. They tend to remember their dreams in remarkable detail. This subject matter can roll over into their waking time producing phobias or paranoia. Drugs also play their part in upsetting sleep with quite a few inhibiting the natural REM patterns; this applies to both vital medication as well as drug abuse. Again, subjects remain in the very deep Delta levels and, do not appear to benefit from this. Dream patterns are also disturbed when weaning subjects off drugs with an increase

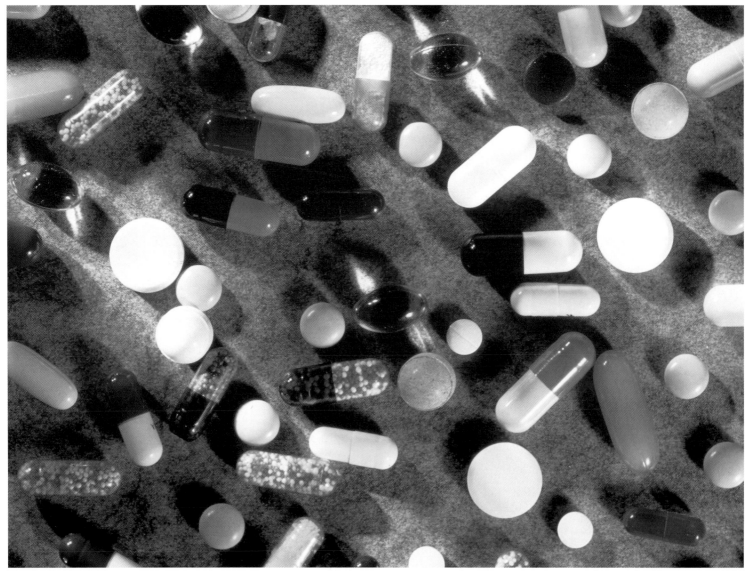

Drugs play their part in upsetting sleep inhibiting natural REM patterns.

in nightmares and anxiety dreams.

Post-Traumatic Stress Disorder (PTSD) is a condition that is becoming more familiar and understood. In this category you will find the victims of war, terrorism, kidnapping, solitary confinement, rape, sexual abuse, natural disasters, and serious accidents. Many show signs of sleep disturbance in the form of nightmares or loss of normal dreaming and REM sleep.

Many schools of thought insist that a part of us, known as the astral body, (the etheric, the dream body, the subtle body, the soul, the spirit, the ghost), actually leaves the physical body when we fall asleep. This is known as an out-of-body experience, or OBE. The astral body can travel vast distances and it is in this state that we frequently experience our

flying dreams. It can also be forced out through accident, anaesthesia, shock, drink, drugs or pain, in fact, any condition where the body becomes unconscious. Think of the expressions we use: "he's passed out; beside himself; out to lunch; spaced out; knocked out; not all here; a screw loose" – all suggest a separation of the mental and physical selves.

There are, of course, certain classic cases, such as when an image of a person appears to a loved one at the moment of death. Many of these instances were documented during wartime. Other instances are when the wraith (the visible spirit, an apparition) is seen leaving the body after death. Scientists have developed various machines which prove that there is an electromagnetic field

or aura around the human body. The most famous is the Kirlian camera which very clearly photographs the first vibrational level of the aura which is said to have seven layers including the physical. All have been seen by gifted clairvoyants. One can perhaps compare them with the layers of atmosphere around the earth, which we accept unquestioningly. The earth's layers are known as the troposphere, the stratosphere, the chemosphere, the ionosphere and the exosphere. Around the human body are the etheric that follows the outline of the body; the astral, the emotional, the mental, the intuitional, the spiritual. Clairvoyants claim to see this field as a multi-colored egg shape, tapering end uppermost, around the body.

The astral body is difficult to

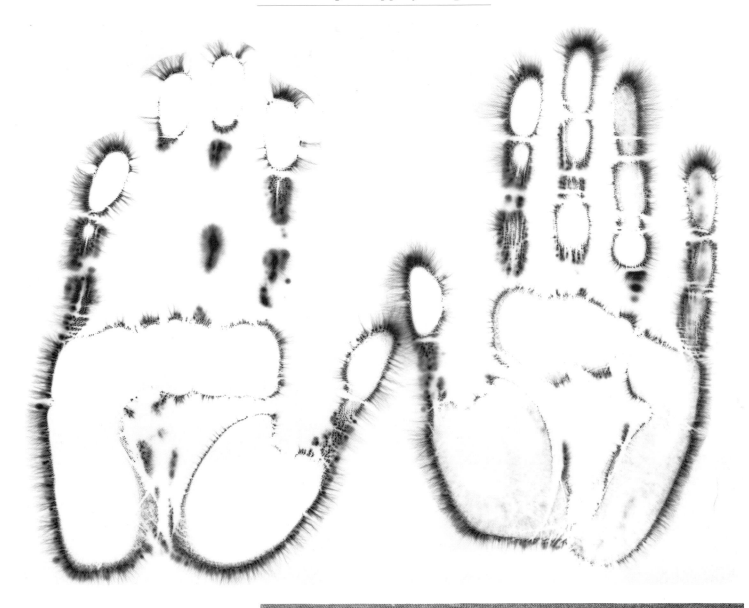

Above: Kirlian photograph of the author's hands showing the first layer of the aura.

Right: The astral body leaves the physical in sleep and we often experience flying dreams.

define, almost behaving like an elementary particle, in that when we try to observe it directly, it cannot be seen. We can only be conscious of its effects. To get a true image of it, we need to look a little to one side of an object and allow our eyes to go fuzzy or slightly out of focus. Again, returning to the world of physics, it is reminiscent of Heisenberg's Uncertainty Principle which showed that one can never be exactly sure of both the position and velocity of a particle simultaneously, since it is impossible to obtain an accurate assessment of one aspect while examining the other. This provoked

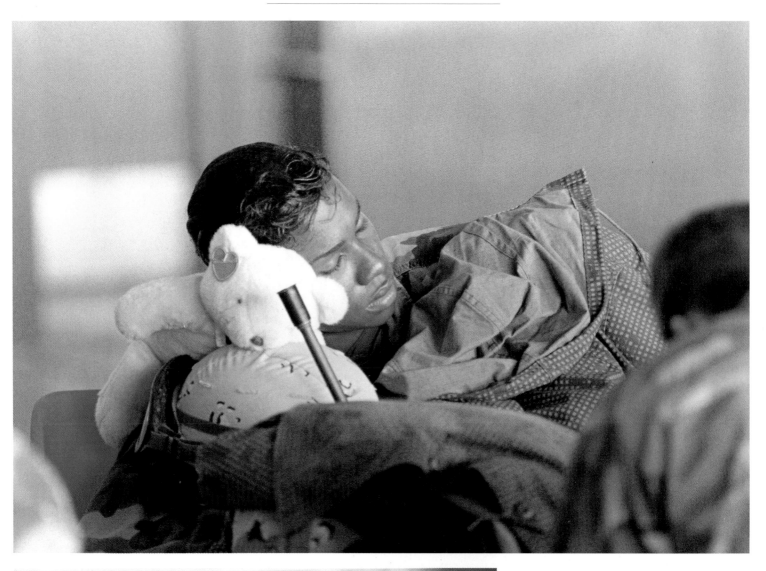

Above: A protection from PTSD, a young sergeant sleeps with her teddy waiting for the UN deadline in Iraq.

Left: An unsettling image of lost souls in the underworld.

a comment from Sir Arthur Eddington that, "Something unknown is doing we don't know what."

As yet there seems to be no theory on whether it is the aura, or a part of the aura, which departs nightly or leaves the body in an OBE, or whether it is something else entirely. What is agreed upon, however, by those who "see" is that it closely resembles the physical and is connected to the sleeping body by a silver cord.

There are several factors which give credence to this departure theory. Firstly, there are now many examples of OBEs particularly the flush of good documentation on "near death experiences". So very many people have described being out of their bodies, having no physical sensations but being able to hear and observe. It is a clear sensation of inhabiting a consciousness that is quite separate from one's physical state. Descriptions of medical operations together with conversations among the medical staff are multitudinous. Research is currently taking place where objects are secretly put out of sight in high positions in the operating theater to try to validify the statements. Straightforward out of body experiences are also well documented. I, myself, have had such an experience. I was aware that I was sitting on top of the wardrobe which was, in fact, impossible since there was insufficient room. I was looking down on the sleeping forms of myself and my two room mates. The moment was brief, but extremely clear.

There is another documented form of OBE, that of bi-location. In these instances the body is functioning equally well in two localities simultaneously which puts one in mind of the EPR (Einstein, Podolski and Rosen) theory of non-locality. Two interacting particles are separated by great distances. A measurement made on one simultaneously affects the outcome of the measurements made on the other. Here is a recorded case: "A bishop was participating at a conference at the Vatican in which he was very involved, whilst at the same time he was at home attending the sick bed of one of his flock. He was seen simultaneously at both places."

Sudden awakenings or disturbances cause the astral to return to the sleeping body at great speed. This gives rise, in the dream state, to a sensation of falling or crashing, often resulting in a nasty ending to the dream. Sometimes there is a misalignment causing that ghastly out of

Simulated misalignment of the aura. Shadowing effect is similar to the etheric or first layer.

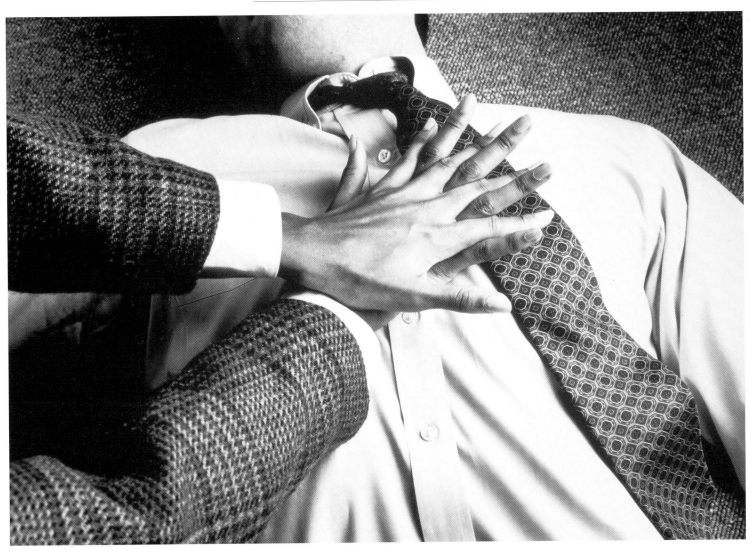

A near-death experience: this is often the time when out of body experiences occur.

sorts sensation with headaches, nausea and general grogginess on awakening. The best cure is to turn over and return to sleep, but so rarely can we indulge ourselves that we often have to endure several hours before we thoroughly feel "ourselves" again. Misalignment can also occur following any loss of consciousness from anaesthetics to coma. Many healers have discovered that in the latter case it appears that the astral is afraid to return to the physical having been forced out with such violence. They find encouraging it back is rather like enticing a timid animal and full alignment cannot always be obtained. Maybe this has something to do with semi-paralysis and spasticism.

There are people who consciously practise separating the astral from

Left: Visitations.

the physical. They are aware of rising up and gazing down on their inert bodies before departing to any place of their choosing. This is not a true dream state and has been considerably researched under laboratory conditions in both the USA and Russia in the hope that the method could be used for spying. They hoped that a conscious "astral" could enter a foreign environment and, for example, open safes containing state secrets.

Where does the astral body go each night? There are many theories. The main one is that each one of us needs to review our waking time by taking an overview. This is the dream period. Rising in this manner allows us to see the day and our lives as a whole and is why sometimes we see into the future. If you take the example of Nelson's Column in London, when we are at ground level in

Trafalgar Square, we are mostly conscious of the lions and the pigeons. However, if we climb a little way up the column we can see further afield. If we were to sit on the top with Nelson himself we would be able to see over a wide distance. We would be able to see all manner of things about to happen as traffic and people went about their daily business. We could even see accidents about to happen, but would be unable to do anything to prevent them.

Other theories are that we go journeying. This can be simply for the fun of it or for healing or rescue work. There is evidence to show that people have been cured over great distances through a visit from some kind of healer. Other dreamers tell of going on rescue missions, visiting people in great need or dire distress and supporting them through their crises.

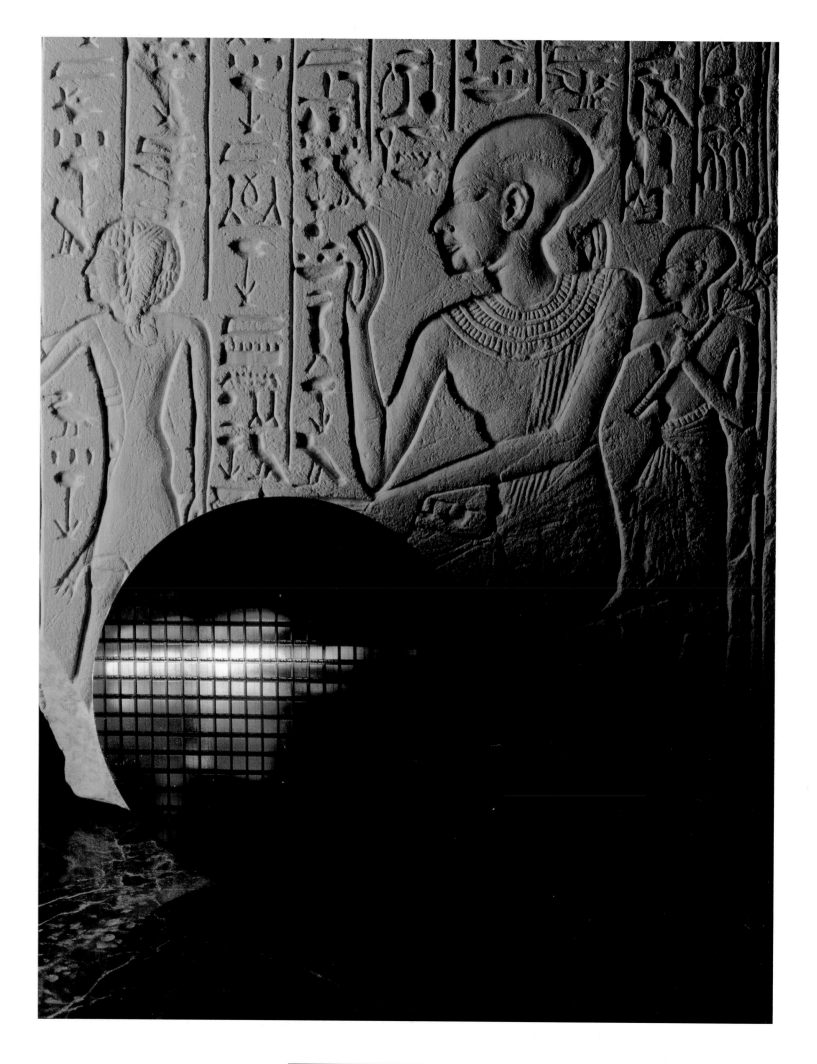

Chapter Four

TYPES AND PURPOSE OF DREAMS

I n the course of this book, I have decided to use the terms conscious and unconscious when describing the mind to avoid confusion. The sub-conscious is synonymous with the unconscious as is the super conscious to the higher self. The dream state has been the source of great literature and many scientific discoveries. It has warned of disasters and saved lives. It is also responsible for changing the course of living for the better for those who pay attention. There are very many categories of dreams and defining their character should be one of our first priorities on interpretation. Let us start with those that are not really dreams.

DAYDREAMS AND REVERIES
We drift into daydreams or reveries during our waking hours and these should be considered as altered states of consciousness (ASCs). "Those who dream by day are cognisant of many things which escape those who dream only by night." (Edgar Allan Poe). It is the deepening Alpha stage moving into light

Opposite: We may have traveled from the hieroglyphic to the computer chip but our dreams still hold the keys.

Theta. We are completely absorbed in a fantasy world which can be extremely emotive. This is also the area of the mind accessed through meditation, either when looking for the empty inner space or path working. Wordsworth's description of daffodils is one of the most evocative:

"When oft upon my couch I lie,
In vacant or in pensive mood,
They flash upon that inward eye,
Which is the bliss of solitude."

Visualization is slightly different in that it is more deliberate and directed. Here we draw upon imagery to suit the circumstances. Listening to radio is a good example as is personal performance enhancement or self-healing.

The most classic example of the results of reverie is that of Archimedes who, "dozing" in his bath suddenly understood the principle of buoyancy. He leapt out and ran naked through the streets shouting "Eureka". Thomas Edison, who invented the phonograph and the incandescent lamp, believed so strongly in reverie, the semi-conscious state, that he kept a cot in his laboratory in which he could relax

and meditate. He actually held a ball in his hand to prevent his falling asleep. If his hand relaxed in sleep, the ball fell onto a metal plate awakening him. Albert Einstein seemed to spend much of his waking hours in the alpha state using it for solving complex mathematical problems. His major discovery dream is detailed later. To quote the French entomologist, Jean Fabre, who always slept on problems, "a brilliant beacon flares up in my brain, and then I jump from my bed, light my lamp and write down the solution, the memory of which would otherwise be lost."

Hypnogogic and hypnopompic images occur in that period between sleeping and waking, hypnogogic as we fall asleep and hypnopompic as we awaken. This is the deep Alpha/light Theta level that is approaching and moving into the Theta level and can often occur in deep meditation. In this state we receive vivid, highly-colored, but seemingly unconnected images. Unknown faces are common, disconnected scenes, altogether rather like a bizarre slide-show. Sometimes the meaning of these can be extremely profound and visionary, but frequently they appear to have

Left: Bizarre and impossible images received in the dream state.

no coherent or valuable message. This state should not be muddled with hallucinations which occur while awake and are a confusion of fantasy images with normal perception. One of the strange things about this type of experience is that we are sure that we are still wide awake and it comes as a surprise to realize that this is not the case. There is a detached feeling about them in which we are not involved, even when they are unpleasant or weird. It is rather like flipping through TV programs with a remote control. It is the world of surrealism.

Examination of the works of great artists gives us some concept of these images. Salvador Dali truly captures the weirdness of the hypnogogic with his strange treatment of everyday objects, veritable dream worlds. This is repeated in the obscure humor of the cartoons of Monty Python. There is a feeling of obsession and extremes. There is a similar nightmarish quality about the work of M C Escher. Superficially, his pictures are interesting structures. Then you find that the staircases disappear, the pathways become a labyrinth, and the viewer is led into the void. Max Ernst, on the other hand, uses archetypal symbology, disproportion and inappropriate juxtapositions.

However, they need not always be weird. One night as I was dropping off, I was trying to fit a tree in my secret garden, which is actually a windswept clifftop. I was choosing something appropriate like a windswept thorn bush, when this was snatched away and replaced by an enormous bare-branched ash tree, literally like a projector chang-

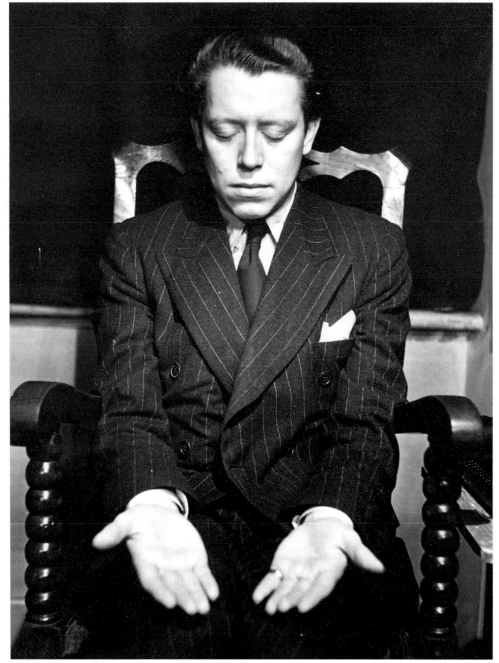

Left: A well-known healer in an altered state of consciousness receiving profound information from his guide.

Opposite: Salvador Dali, the master painter of the hypnogogic and hypnopompic type of images.

The terrifying images of the dream world.

ing the slide. It gave me quite a shock. This had an important meaning for me.

Literal dreams are those that seem to be a review or a continuation of whatever has happened to us during the day. The main point that distinguishes them is the lack of symbolism. Often we refuse to accept a dream at face value and spend many hours trying to read something into it which isn't there. For example, I dreamt I was going out and could not find my car keys. After a prolonged search, I found them on the hook where they should have been. It would be easy to try to read special meanings into this dream, but the truth of the matter is that this is exactly what happens to me on many occasions.

Literal dreams are logical and excessively normal and are the product of our intellect rather than our intuition. They reflect the outside world like a direct photograph rather than a creative composition. They are often an action replay, as above, which gives us the opportunity to review and find other ways of doing things.

Wish fulfilment dreams were the basis of much of the work of Sigmund Freud. We no longer set so much store by them as he did. They are remarkably common and do not carry great depths of meaning. Examples of these are being with a lover or ex-lover, winning large sums of money, holidaying in some tropical place, being famous. In many ways, they are an extension of day

dreaming. We must be careful, however, not to dismiss them since there is just a chance that they are trying to communicate more than the ordinary. If they keep recurring, we should then ask ourselves about our needs to live outside reality.

Compensatory dreams are a strange category of dreaming which closely resembles wish fulfilment. It was discovered that concentration camp inmates rarely had bad dreams or any sort of nightmare. Their dream worlds were full of magic, beauty and pleasant environments, peopled by healthy and happy individuals. The theory is that these dreams compensated for their appalling experiences in their waking hours. Another example of this is the reverse. The wife of a Jewish professor who had everything she could want in life kept having recurring, frightening dreams about the death of her son and husband in some dreadful ordeal. No amount of ordinary interpretation came up with any solution and it was felt that she had tapped into the collective unconscious for these dreams to compensate for her guilt about her current rich lifestyle. They could, of course, have also been far memory dreams.

Serial dreams are not so common but take on the form of a soap opera. Each night produces a new instalment and some subjects simply cannot wait to get to bed to find out what happens next. Sometimes several sequences occur in the same night with waking periods in between. These serials can last one night or several months and, historically, have produced some great novels. One of the most telling examples is that of the Czech novelist, Franz Kafka, who based all his novels on the dream world. They are nightmarish and terrifying and are the result of regular dream sequences, which were fully documented in his diaries. Graham Greene also used this serial form of dreaming for inspiration, often waking several times during the night to continue the storyline and develop the plot of his novels. He kept a dream diary and used its ideas. He is quoted as saying "If I'm really working, I re-read what I've written during the day before I go to bed and the problems are solved in my sleep."

Some serial dreams can cover a lifetime. Hetty Hay-Davies had a series which started in early childhood and were related to her fear of her mother. She had a nightmare of being in a tower and being chased down a spiral staircase by an unseen monster through small rooms filled with furniture. Her fear of her mother obviously manifested as the monster and she felt trapped in her environment. Later on having left home, she dreamt of being in a Victorian house, which had something evil in the attic. She made contact with a monk who sent some investigators to deal with the problem. The evil spirits gathered to attack and she returned to the kitchen where everything was light and bright. She had a tremendous shock when she met herself. Here she had escaped the earlier influences and moved into a greater personal space. However, she had not rid herself entirely of her

earlier fears which still need exorcising. The kitchen is the place of nourishment and here is filled with the light of enlightenment. Thus she meets herself, since it is she, herself, who is the barrier to her freedom from fear.

Many years later after her mother had died, she dreamt again of re-visiting a tower/house, which was now derelict with a companion. They climbed to the attic and found a dream lover being kept by the daughter of the house to whom it owed its existence. This lover turned out to be a cardboard effigy, with which the daughter was deceiving herself. The companion picked it up and flew away with it. This dream clearly shows how Hetty had been fostering this fear within herself in the form of a lover, she had become so attached to it. However, her guide took it away, since once recognized, it was no longer needed. It clearly shows that she was still clinging to the past. The next dream shows Hetty clearing out her parents' house. She comes across her mother wearing a silly, frilly pink dress and looking very childish, not like her real self.

Here it is clear her fears are finally exorcised and she sees her mother in her true light. These dreams spanned 50 years.

Many great writers, poets, artists and musicians have developed their work in and from the dream state. Robert Louis Stevenson is a case in point. Complete stories came to him this way. Those known to be the result of dreams are *The Strange Case of Dr Jekyll and Mr Hyde*, *Treasure Island* and *Across the Plains*. As his health failed he dropped more and more into the dreaming. He describes how he found the plot for *Dr Jekyll & Mr Hyde*: "For two days I went about racking my brains for a plot of any sort; and on the second night I dreamed the scene at the window, and a scene afterwards split in two, in which Hyde, pursued for some crime, took a powder and underwent the change in the presence of his pursuers." Stevenson also used to tell himself stories before he went to sleep which were then amplified in

When life is hard we resort to wish fulfilment and compensatory dreams.

"dreams which stayed with me ever after and changed my ideas; they have gone through and through me, like wine through water, and altered the colour of my mind." One of the most lyrical comments is from the great Irish poet, William Butler Yeats

"But I, being poor, have only my dreams;
I have spread my dreams under your feet;
Tread softly, because you tread on my dreams."

In the musical field, many well-known composers are said to have been inspired by their dreams. Some, such as Beethoven, Schumann, Mozart, and Ravel, actually heard bits of the music which they recalled on waking. Guiseppe Tartini wrote *The Devil's Sonata* following an incredibly vivid dream about Satan playing his violin, and Elgar's *Dream of Gerontius* is based on a poem by Cardinal John Newman that originated from a dream.

Above: Robert Louis Stevenson at his desk – a great believer in dreams as a source of inspiration.

Right: Lewis Carroll, the creator of the surrealist tales, Alice in Wonderland & Through the Looking Glass.

the dream state.

John Bunyan, author of *The Pilgrim's Progress* stated of his writing ". . . and as I slept, I dreamed a dream." Walter de la Mare was another dreamer, as was the Russian novelist, Fyodor Dostoyevsky. In *The Brothers Karamazov*, Ivan meets the Devil in a dream. *Alice in Wonderland* and other novels of Lewis Carroll are very clearly the result of the author's dreaming. In this instance many of the images are remarkably archetypal and symbolic. Her trip through the looking-glass is a clear example of moving into another dimension, such as in a dream. Emily Bronte used dreams to add greater color to her writing and her Cathy in *Wuthering Heights* had

The writer drawing inspiration from his dreams.

Symbolic dreams form the main body of dreaming. Some theorists consider them to be devoid of a plot. They are the true messages from our unconscious minds to our waking minds. It would appear that the unconscious is not capable of working through logic and thus uses images which represent situations and feeling as a descriptive language.

Each one of us has our own language developed since birth from our personal life experiences, our own hieroglyphics. Thus a mother is not necessarily a caring, nurturing person since for one dreamer a mother may represent being devoured because his mother over-loved him, or for another she may represent neglect because that was his experience. Care should always be exercised before offering any general or archetypal explanation. When a person cannot come up with any coherent interpretation which means something then we resort to these broader meanings which

reside in the collective unconscious.

Here is a symbolic dream of mine from the age of five: "When I was quite small I had a dream that I went with my aunt, because there was a special celebration, to a cave on a headland which was part of the local golf course. We stood on the edge of a large sinkhole which goes through to the sea and watched a drama with a sinuous woman completely clothed in a body suit of green sequins." What is interesting here is that I was quite convinced that this experience had actually happened, but whenever I mentioned it to my aunt or my sister, both looked at me blankly, having no recollection what-soever of the incident. I was over 40 when it eventually dawned on me that this was a dream (I think?), because the whole thing was physi-cally impossible. It is still clear today.

Nightmares result from two sources. Firstly, they can be the sur-facing brain's interpretation of an actual physical state – sleep paraly-

sis, myoclonic jerks, external noises, sudden awakenings. Secondly, they are brought on by suppression of all our doubts and fears that we are unable to face up to during the day. Falling and being chased are very common.

So many frightening images can be invoked from our own experience and the collective cultural experi-ence which are portrayed around us in art, literature and the media. If we look at paintings by the early reli-gious artists showing their interpre-tations of hell and demons, it is hard-ly surprising that we use these crea-tures to scare ourselves. And, how about films such as *Psycho* and *Frankenstein*?

Again, we need to look back to past experiences to discover why our unconscious minds have chosen certain images. All the monsters, bogeymen, and threatening people are synonymous with those around us either at work, or among our friends, or in the home. These need to be confronted and handled, which

Above: James Watt, the Scottish inventor whose recurring dreams of raining lead pellets led to the creation of ball bearings.

Left: Elias Howe, the American inventor, whose nightmares solved the problem of the locking stitch in sewing machines.

often takes courage. Until they are, the nightmares will continue. It is easy to see, therefore, that recurring dreams and nightmares indicate that we are not dealing with our problems in life. Sometimes it is difficult to recognize the repeating problem in our waking circumstances because different people and places may be involved in our dreams. The dream mind, however, very definitely recognizes the repeat scenario and throws it up for us to become more aware, to extricate ourselves and stop making the same mistakes.

Sometimes nightmares are of some use. James Watt, a Scottish inventor and engineer, had a recurring dream that he was walking through a rain storm of heavy lead

pellets rather like hail stones. He eventually realized that if molten lead is dropped from a great height it forms spheres, and invented ball-bearings.

Another well-documented nightmare is that of Elias Howe who invented the sewing machine. He was having trouble creating the locking stitch. He dreamt he had been captured by natives who all carried spears which had holes through the blades. He realized that the position for the eye of the needle was at the point, and went on to produce the machine needles we know today.

How is it possible to see into the future? Well, we really don't yet have conclusive answers. We touched on one possibility in

Chapter 3, that of astral traveling or of being out of our bodies. Precognition is knowing about something in advance; a premonition is a warning in advance, a foreboding, (we do not necessarily know exactly what is going to happen). Precognitive dreams about disasters of major proportions are well documented. Before the Aberfan disaster in Wales in 1966, many people dreamed of the moving slurry hill and the enveloped schoolyard. My own grandmother dreamed of the 1906 San Francisco earthquake, and the Agadir earthquake of 1960 was foreseen by many dreamers. Other disasters such as the sinking of the *Titanic*, assassinations of presidents and prime ministers, railway or aeroplane crashes have all appeared in precognitive dreams.

As a young corporal on the Somme during the First World War, Adolf Hitler had a nightmare that he was being suffocated by falling earth and debris. On awakening the dream was so vivid that he felt he could not breathe so he ran outside. Within minutes a shell landed on the bunker and killed all the occupants: a clear instance of a dream changing the face of history. A similar story is told about how Bismarck had many dreams which guided him to victory.

Another strange area of precognitive dream is that of knowing details and facts that should be completely outside our ken. An exponent of this type of dreaming is Chris Robinson, who currently helps the British police solve crimes. On one occasion he dreamed of his wedding day and an image of a high fence linked with disaster. On awakening, he remembered that this fence surrounded a military establishment and knew the dream was about a bomb. He warned the necessary authorities, who naturally thought he was mad. However, he was proved right. He has had other dreams where he has found lost people and hidden corpses and is now taken seriously. Geroge Cranley, used to dream of race winners on a regular basis, and made sufficient funds to bring himself and a col-

Adolf Hitler whose First World War nightmare saved his life.

league to Britain from South Africa. Another young man who had been considering suicide, having lost all his money on horses and being unable to honor his debts, was saved by the dream of a friend of another winning horse.

With premonitions, we are clearly being warned about some future danger, which, of course, we are quite at liberty to ignore. Our dreams are giving us the option to make a change to those things that we can change and to prepare for those we can't. If a death dream is

truly about a death, then when it happens in reality, we have already had the opportunity to get over the shock and the experience is easier to handle. It also makes us of more use to others for this reason and we can be a real support to them in their time of crisis. Examples of this are the dreams, usually of mothers or girlfriends under conditions of war or extreme stress, of having seen their sons, boyfriends or husbands standing in the room with them. Subsequent investigations usually prove that this experience coincided

So very frequently major disasters are dreamed of in advance.

with the moment of death.

In my own experience I had a dream to take care when driving. I naturally thought of accidents. The following day I was late as usual, driving to an appointment. The route I took had at least six sets of traffic lights. At each set a little voice within said "take the cross country route, turn right." On each occasion I ignored it, feeling that the main road would be longer, but quicker. Eventually, with great relief, I was able to drop a gear and speed up. Two minutes later I was stopped at a police speed trap. Well, I couldn't say I hadn't been warned!

Denise Linn in her book, *A Pocketful of Dreams* has some useful pointers for precognitive dreams.

She makes the following suggestions:

1. The dream is in color or the colors are unusually vivid. A precognitive dream isn't always in color, but it can be one of several determining factors.

2. You will get the message in three different ways during the dream. The message will appear in three separate, but distinct forms within one dream.

3. There will usually be a round or circular object within the dream. This can be an object such as a ball, a plate or a circular mirror.

Sometimes we experience what are known as "far-memory" dreams. These are dreams of past lives, of having lived before in a different period. We may find ourselves of a different gender and age. They are identified by their clarity and general simplicity. Whilst they are not very common, they do tend to create strong and lasting impressions.

How do we know it is a past life? The answer is: we don't. It is sensible, therefore, always to test our memory banks before getting too excited. It is always possible that we have read or heard about the situation before, which invalidates the dream from the far-memory category. We do not know what prompts them, unless we have been specifically exploring such a possibility.

My own experience was an extremely brief dream, several years ago. I was a priest in a temple-type of building with two others, one of whom was my helper and the other the patient. There was a stone couch. I knew we had to lie on the couch with the patient between us, my helper protecting. We had to sleep and I would meet the patient in the dream state and heal him. At this time, I knew absolutely nothing about Asclepius and the healing dream temples and was quite taken aback when informed. It is ironical but it has only just struck me that my current work is healing through dreams!

Déjà vu is a waking experience where we feel we have seen the whole view or experienced a situation on a previous occasion. It is a clear repeat. It is frequently equated with having dreamed, but not consciously remembered. Whilst this is totally possible, there can be other explanations such as a forgotten early memory or a past life experience. Recording our dreams helps to identify some of the possibilities. There are several documented cases of children confidently leading adults around venues which none of them have ever visited before. Did they have a precognitive dream or is it a far-memory? Several books with extremely good factual, historical detail have been written from far memory recall.

There is another area which should be addressed and that is the one of visions. These are views of the future that have an inspirational aspect. The implications are less immediate and more idealistic. Perhaps the most well-known is Joan of Arc, whose dream was to save France from the English. One cannot be sure, of course, whether she was in reverie, meditation or dream. Another documented dreaming visionary was René Descartes, the French philosopher and proponent of "I think, therefore, I am." Descartes had a series of three dreams which were the outcome of extreme concentration and the seeding of all his accumulated knowledge. The result was the idea to construct a complete science of nature which would have absolute certainty, that "all science is certain, evident knowledge." The philosophy of Descartes has had a profound influence on modern thinking up until the present, in that it is responsible for the separation of mind and body into individual units.

Historically, there have been many such visionaries who tune into the dream world. Over 500 years ago, Leonardo da Vinci designed an aeroplane and a submarine; and who knows whether the wilder fantasies of science fiction writers will come true?

INCUBATED AND PROBLEM SOLVING DREAMS

The process of sowing an idea in our minds just as we fall asleep; the old fashioned idea of "sleeping on a problem" often gives rise to a problem-solving dream. Invariably, in the morning we have the answer, or it occurs to us later in the day. In the majority of cases, this is completely spontaneous. By taking control of this process, incubating, or seeding as it is often called, can be made into

Above: René Descartes, the French philosopher, who incubated his dreams to enable him to construct a science of absolute certainty.

Right: Prince Leopold von Bismarck-Shoenhausen who used his dreams to assist his battle strategies.

Can we influence people's dreams to cause them to act outside their normal behavior?

one of the most valuable aspects of dreaming. To do this, we need to make a deliberate point of sowing the seed and *asking* for an answer, (some people write a note to themselves and place it under the pillow). In the morning, it is vital to give our full attention to discovering any response, because it can come in so many forms.

Here are some outstanding examples of "sleeping on it". Professor Freidrich Kekule von Stradonitz, a German chemist, was desperate to discover the molecular structure of a particular chemical. He received the answer in a dream as he was dozing by the fire: "the atoms were gamboling before my eyes. . . . the smaller groups kept in the background. My mental eye, rendered more acute by repeated visions of this kind, could now distinguish larger structures, of manifold confirmation; long rows, sometimes more closely fitted together; all twining and twisting in snakelike motion. But look! What

was that? One of the snakes had seized hold of its own tail and the form whirled mockingly before my eyes. As if in a flash of lightning, I awoke." Professor Kekule recognized this symbol as being the answer to his difficulty and thus the knowledge of the benzene ring came into being.

What is interesting here is that he mentions "repeated visions". Could it be that the answer had been available on a number of occasions but his waking mind had not registered the fact? Most of our answers are around us. It is crucial to listen to the still, small voice, but not to be governed by it. *Learn discrimination.* Anyway, as a result, the professor's comment to his learned friends was "Gentlemen, learn to dream."

Another famous dreamer was Napoleon, who used his dreams to plan his battle strategies. On waking he created action models to confirm their viability.

Albert Einstein acknowledged

that his theory of relativity was the result of a childhood dream. He dreamt that he was speeding downhill on a sledge going so fast that he was approaching the speed of light. This speed created visual distortions so that when he looked at the sky, the stars and planets were transformed with many different patterns and colors. He is said to have based all of his future work on this dream.

The archaeologist Herman Hilprecht was struggling to decipher the script on some fragments of what he thought were agate rings, without any success. On falling asleep he was visited by a temple priest who informed him of the meaning of the inscription and that the pieces were actually part of a pair of earrings.

False awakening is an interesting condition in which we are asleep and dreaming, but think that we are awake. There are many examples; for instance, a friend dreamt that she was getting up in the morning, going through the whole routine of dressing, eating and leaving for work only to wake up and find that none of this had actually happened. Other examples occur when napping. We believe we have woken and are continuing with our day, often achieving quite important feats, only to awake and find we haven't even started. This is the stage that often immediately precedes lucid dreaming and when recognized can lead us into this state.

Lucid dreams or dreaming true has been the subject of extensive research. It is when you are asleep and dreaming and actually know that you are asleep and dreaming within the dream state. I recall my son telling me of a dream where he was walking on sand, freshly washed smooth by the receding tide, when he came across some strange signs scored on the surface. While he was looking at them, he became aware that he was in the dream state and that he had to memorize these inscriptions to tell me about them when he awoke. As he was describing his dream to me, he drew what he had seen. They were runic symbols with a message that there would be trouble with a partnership. This turned out to be true for me at work.

Through this sort of awareness, it is possible to control and direct the sequence of events. In other words, you can change the outcome. This is particularly valuable in the case of nightmares or anything that is mildly threatening. Dr. Stephen LeBerge of Stanford University says of lucid dreaming that "it is like having a personal laboratory or playground for trying out new behaviors and ways of being." It introduces us to that part of ourselves which creates dreaming. This, in turn, allows us to become more conscious in our daily activities and also to create our futures by exploring all the possible outcomes in the dream state. From time to time this will involve others whom we know, so a high ethical standard should be observed.

Whilst agreeing that altering nightmares can bring about real relief, I would first postulate that when you dream, your unconscious mind is trying to tell you something. It is important, therefore, first of all to realize what that message is and take the necessary action if you can, to improve your circumstances. If you practice lucid dreaming and start altering many of your dreams, surely you are missing important messages and merely developing a fantasy world or playground for your own imagination. On the other hand, one must consider the argument that initially one has become lucid spontaneously and this, in itself, must have its own value. The whole purpose of arriving at this point is to make the appropriate alterations and possibly re-program the unconscious mind. One more uncharted function of the brain is gradually emerging.

The false awakening effect can be a guide into participating in the dream. Lucid dreams are often preceded by sensations of flying or floating, and a clear knowledge that you are dreaming. Dr Keith Hearne has done considerable research on training people to dream lucidly and he identifies a number of clear clues which he calls "ten tests for state-assessment."

1. Switch on an electric light in the dream. If it does not work, or there is a malfunction of any kind, or you cannot find it, suspect very strongly that you are dreaming. This applies to any electrical appliance.

2. Attempt to "float" in mid-air or fly. Success is proof of dreaming.

3. Jump off an object, such as a chair. If you descend slowly, then you know you are dreaming.

4. Look carefully at your surroundings. Is there anything there which is incongruous?

5. Look at your body and your clothes. Is this *your* body and are the clothes yours in waking life?

6. Look out of the window. Is the environment accurate? Is the season correct, and is the light-level right for the time?

7. Attempt to alter a detail in the scenery, or make something happen by will-power.

8. Attempt to push your hand through solid-looking objects.

9. Pinch your skin. Is the texture as it should be?

10. Look in a mirror. Is there some alteration to your face.

If most of these points pertain to your dream then you are lucid. Most of your environment will be perfectly normal, but with small inconsistencies together with a sense of

Dr. Friedrich Kekule von Stradonitz, the German chemist who discovered the benzene ring after dreaming about snakes.

Albert Einstein, the physicist, famous for his theory of relativity which he claims came to him as a result of a dream.

being invisible. You are able to become your own "film director" and become thoroughly creative.

We can use incubation or dream seeding in conjunction with lucidity. Here we can direct the solution to a given problem so that the outcome is truly comfortable. Take a phobia, for example, a fear of spiders. In the lucid dream we can either grow in size so that the spider disappears into insignificance or we can reduce the spider until it is barely visible. In either case our fears can be eliminated. We can also use seeding for healing. In the lucid state we can discover the absolutely correct medicine for our needs.

There is another form of dreaming that, to date, is still in the realms of science fiction, that of a trained lucid dreamer entering the dreams of another and controling and radically altering his dreams. By the use of suggestion, he can influence that person to commit acts outside his normal behavior. These theories are the basis of a novel called *Dreamscape* which was made into a quite terrifying film.

Dreamsharing occurs between people who are very close to each other either physically, in the same bed, or mentally and emotionally. In this instance both parties participate simultaneously in the same dream. This is not all that common.

A friend who was having a dispute with her partner dreamt that she was dancing at a disco to the tune of *Eleanor Rigby.* Her partner dreamt he was at a Beatles concert, tapping his feet in time to the music. The tune was *Eleanor Rigby*! In other words, they were dancing to the same tune, but not together.

My husband and I had been exploring lots of standing stones and were curious about their purpose. That night he dreamt that he was peering through an eyelet in the rock face up a narrow cleft with an intensely red sky, whilst I dreamt that I was on a river flowing through a deep narrow valley made of red rocks.

"My mother dreamt she was getting married to an old family friend, who was very neatly dressed and looked well. On the same night the family friend's daughter also dreamt that he was getting married but she did not know to whom. In her dream he was also neatly dressed and looked well." These are clearly sharing and synchronistic dreams. It would seem that the family friend is entering into some sort of contract or commitment which is important enough to get dressed up for and looking well shows it to be healthy. Both the mother and the daughter could be aware of this and the mother's closer connection could mean that it was her suggestion originally. If you are a member of a group, especially one meditating or exploring dreams, it can happen that a common dream theme will emerge.

Hypnotic dreams come in two categories. Firstly, there are those which are seeded during the therapy session and occur away from the consulting room during a normal night's sleep. Hypnotherapists can help us to pinpoint the area in our psyche which is demanding attention. Armed with this new knowledge and with the post-hypnotic suggestions implanted during the therapy, this seeding exercise is invaluable. There can also be a spontaneous dream response to post-hypnotic suggestion which should be addressed by the therapist at future sessions. This can often confuse a client if not shared and explained. Another feature of hypnosis is that it can stimulate memories of earlier dreams and give a clue to an experience which, although unrecognized, is being repeated. The second form is that of bringing a dream to the therapist which can be further explored under hypnosis. Perhaps it is unfinished, so with gentle guidance, we can be led to the conclusion. Care must be observed here though that the therapist does not superimpose outside theories into our dream.

A fairly usual form of hypnotherapy is regression, usually to point of birth or conception. However, this can trigger the unconscious mind to explore further and throw up clear past life memories in the dream state. Regression, therefore, should not be undertaken lightly and only with an experienced exponent.

Healing dreams occur in several ways. Firstly, those which state the condition of the body: plumbing, for example relates to the urinary system, flat tyres to the respiratory system etc. Secondly, there are the dreams of medicines or items on shelves, of being in the kitchen, which shows a need to feed ourselves. Thirdly, there are the dream visitors who come when we are actually ill and either recommend a treatment or actually give it themselves. These can be our guides or guardian angels or else actual healers who are astral traveling (see previous chapter).

There is a documented case of a well known archaeologist being struck down by a virulent fever whilst he was in Egypt. He dreamed that he had been visited by a doctor, dressed in the conventional black coat and striped trousers of the time, who gave him something for his fever. The dream doctor told the patient that he had come from Britain and was often called upon in the dream state. The archaeologist subsequently recovered and on his return home appealed via the radio for such a doctor. A doctor from Scotland came forward and identified himself as the dream helper.

Making the bizarre credible.

Chapter Five

UNDERSTANDING YOUR DREAMS

Understanding your dreams and acting on their advice can change and enhance your life. Once we appreciate the difference between the simple daily reviews or wish fulfillments, to read our own strange language of images, we can begin to hear the messages and advice from our deep unconscious minds. Experience will show that dreams are not so much rubbish but an important area of our lives which, for many, remains untapped.

Rather than produce a dream dictionary, throughout the following chapters we will explore the major dream symbols. These are the subconscious topics around which we weave all our emotions, hopes and fears. Remembering that all our images are our own inventions drawn from our personal experiences, if we take these themes which are the clues, we can then, using our common sense, easily find out how

other, less frequently used, images interweave.

How do I remember my dreams? is the common cry. It is really quite simple but does require dedication and persistence. Firstly, obtain a dream diary. This can be a simple notebook, a tape recorder or dictaphone, or a loose leaf containing pages with the headings shown below. A dictaphone can only be used if you sleep alone or you will

disturb your partner. You will need a torch and a writing implement. The moment you wake you must write anything you can remember, words, colors, impressions. The waking mind releases the night images almost immediately, so any delay can be your undoing. Write down the important features first, because the whole dream will take time to record. Very often we become so absorbed in the detail of the begin-

Right: The dream mind is extremely inventive. This one is about accumulation beginning at the new moon.

Left: The use of imagery to indicate waking dangers. The dreamer needs to learn the skills of the tightrope.

Left: Harold Lloyd is frequently depicted in the hair-raising situations normally only experienced in dreams.

Above: The epitome of voluptuousness, a typical wish fulfillment dream.

ning that we forget that all-important answer to the $64,000 question. A few crucial and pertinent words will help to hold the entire sequence so that you can elaborate at your leisure.

There are several reasons for keeping a dream diary. Firstly, so that you can understand what your dream mind is trying to tell you so you can put it to use, and secondly, to look for the patterns that tend to emerge over a period of time. You may discover that you only have memorable dreams around the full moon, or on the 15th of each month, for example. This is particularly useful if you wish to incubate a dream for an important answer. You can time your request to your most fertile dreaming period. You may find that you have the same dream or one expressing a similar set of circumstances whenever certain situations occur in your life. Thus, when you learn to recognize the pattern, you can deal better with that interview, or confrontation, visit to your mother-in-law or whatever your repeated problem may be. It will make clear to you why it is registering with you. All of our emotions and fears are hid-

The road to success requires concentration on work, the briefcases. It is an uphill struggle to overtake those on the same route.

den in our dream language.

If you feel that you never dream and would like to explore your dream world the procedure is as follows: every night, as you are waiting to fall asleep, concentrate on your desire to remember your dreams. Program your unconscious mind. Tell it that it will remember in the morning. You can write your wish on a piece of paper and place it under your pillow. This is exactly the same method that you use for incubating dreams to answer problems. Then, the moment you wake, write down whatever is in your mind. It doesn't matter how silly it appears to be. It may be slow at first, but don't despair. Even the most reluctant minds have produced the information in the end. Just keep repeating your request each night.

The dream diary overleaf shows the current date and the major occurrences of yesterday and today. These will reveal if the dream is a current answer or worry. It may be just a review, it may be telling you how to deal with what has or what will happen, rather than some overview of the next period in your life. The first thing to write down is the skeleton of what happened in the dream while it is all fresh in your mind. Keep it really brief, because forgetting is almost automatic. Occasionally, dreams remain with you all day or even longer. These occur when the message needs hammering home and the dream mind feels that the conscious mind refuses to acknowledge what it is being shown. Alternatively, they are precognitive or symbolical. Having got the bare bones on paper, you can then elaborate to your heart's content. You will see listed a number of headings which should be completed where relevant if the meaning of the dream is not immediately clear. Explanations of these are found in the succeeding chapters.

The most important thing to realize when trying to interpret dreams is that generally the storyline is only partially to do with the meaning. This is why they frequently seem so bizarre. The reason is that virtually every image in a dream means something else. A father is not a father, he is a representation of authority or

Right: Remembering the lost fire of youth.

Sleeping alone – an example of a pun. The dreamer sees herself as old and unwanted.

kindness or protection. The message is in the representative words. Thus if you take the various images and replace them with their hidden meanings, the correct storyline appears.

For example, in my dream I feel hungry so I go to the kitchen. Then the front door bursts open and I am invaded by dogs who, ignoring me, eat up all the food. There is nothing left for me. One interpretation is that there is a need in me. The kitchen is the source of nourishment (or starvation) – either food, love or attention of some sort – and the front door is access from my safe environment to the outside world. Dogs are usually friends. So the dream means that I am feeling neglected and have retreated inside myself but have left the door open for my friends. They come but merely make use of me and what I have to offer rather than giving real friendship so I am still left in need.

The other important factor to look out for is puns. They are often metaphors common to our everyday language, such as "feeling blue" "being crabby" or "dog-in-a-manger." These can appear in dreams as the colors or animals which should be taken both literally and metaphorically.

Some people never have a satisfactory love life in reality. This can lead

to them straying from partnerships, having crushes on those around them, or idol and hero worship from afar. If we wish we can create our perfect dream lover through dream

incubation. Again, follow the seeding process, make notes on all the attributes you would like to find in this person. Draw a picture if you can. Don't use pictures of actual people since it can be possible to make contact in the dream state and, we have no right to invade the lives of others. They rarely live up to our expectations anyway and we could be in for a big disappointment. Instead, select your own special person. The next stage is to set the scene and as you fall asleep, fantasize on the beautiful romantic setting you imagine yourself to be in with your special lover. It does not always work at first, and you can get some unexpected companions, whom you have to send on their way. If this happens, start the whole process all over again from the beginning.

Below: Improve your sex life by creating a dream lover.

DREAM DIARY

Today's Date: _____

Main Event YESTERDAY: _____

NEXT Main Event: _____

BRIEF RESUME OF DREAM: _____

_____

_____

_____

TYPE: Ordinary, Recurring, Serial, Lucid, Precognitive, Nightmare, Incubated, Sexual, Wish fulfilment, Visionary, Other _____

TIME: Past, Present, Future, Day, Night, Dawn, Midday, Evening, Midnight, Spring, Summer, Autumn, Winter, Childhood, Historical, Far Memory, Other _____

JOURNEY: _____

_____

ATMOSPHERE: _____

OWN FEELINGS: _____

BACKGROUND: _____

BUILDINGS: _____

PEOPLE/ANIMALS: _____

OBJECTS: _____

COLORS: _____

SYMBOLS: _____

WORDS: _____

PUNS: _____

Chapter Six

JOURNEYS

One of the major features to look for in our dreams is that of journeying, because this refers to our journey through life. If we look carefully it is almost always present in some form, on land, sea, or in the air. How you are doing it is important.

If we are simply walking along a road in a dream, the meaning is basic and clear. However, how are we walking? I am walking through the forest at an even pace, without hesitation, in a purposeful manner, an upright posture, looking straight ahead I can see where I am going along a straight route.

Let us now take the building blocks of this scenario and study it more closely:

Direction:	straightforward
Pace:	even
Method:	walking
Effort:	easy
Attitude:	confident
Direction of vision:	forward

So, the current path through life is direct with clear goals and we feel confident.

In another dream sequence I am creeping through a forest. The path

Left: The majority of our dreams are about our journey through life, our route to the rainbow, the promised land.

Right: So often we create impossible barriers to our progress.

winds and I cannot see clearly ahead. I have to bend my head to avoid low branches. I am afraid and want to turn back. There is a noise and I hide behind a large oak tree. Applying the same criteria we have the following:

Direction:	winding
Pace:	intermittent
Method:	creeping
Effort:	hesitant
Attitude:	nervous
Direction of vision:	ahead, but obstructed

Here, the journey through life is entirely different. It shows the dreamer is of a nervous disposition, without clear goals, who prefers to hide rather than confront difficulties and so does not put much effort into achieving anything.

Let's consider the different ways of moving. These can all be applied to our life journey. Firstly, how are you moving?

Our dreams show us our self-created dangers. Here our character is on the brink of a steep and rough route guarded by the demon.

Pace	Interpretation
slow	extreme care reluctance
fast	in a hurry/trying to avoid issues
stationary	taking a break/not capable of moving
hurrying	trying to catch up/ getting behind
hesitant	hesitant
erratic	disinterested inconsequential
sliding	take care/out of control/speed
rhythmic	keeping in time/in tune with yourself
marking time	waiting/not making decisions
vibrating	being manipulated being in tune
intermittent	uncommitted/assessing the situation

This list shows personal effort:

Method	Interpretation
walking	no problems
dragging feet/ shuffling	reluctance
crawling	learning/ obsequious/ struggling
creeping	taking great care/ fearful
limping/ on crutches	in need of support
tripping	not looking where you are going
pushing	great personal effort
jogging	jogging along/casual
running	in a hurry/putting in some effort
climbing	putting in effort/ social climbing/ achievement
jumping	clearing obstacles
skipping	happiness/avoiding obstacles
dancing	happiness/in tune with others
falling	out of control/off your perch
flying	taking an overview/ need for earthing
riding/driving	being in control/being taken for a ride
pedaling/ rowing	getting a move on/ putting in effort
swimming	personal effort
diving	going in headlong
wading	making heavy weather
racing	desire to win
chasing	goal seeking/ entrapment
tunneling	going underground/ taking cover
strolling/ sauntering	reckless

A moment of fear. Hemmed in by the light our way ahead is obscured.   *Supervising our defenses can be tiring and arduous work.*

Other methods of journeying provide further interpretations. The important feature of riding is who is in control. Are we in charge or are we being taken for a ride? This point is crucial since so often in life we are being manipulated by others without realizing it. In the animal context it is particularly clear. If you are horseback riding and the horse is galloping off with you or bucking you off, a really powerful energy is at work and you certainly aren't in charge.

In any sort of vehicle the first factor is who is driving, be it on land, sea or in the air? If it is you, then the question is what are you driving and in what manner are you driving? So, let's look at the different vehicles. Vehicles of all varieties represent our personalities and there is clearly a big difference between say, a go-cart and a Ferrari, a rowing boat and an

ocean liner, a hang-glider and a jet fighter. It is quite remarkable how much information can be gleaned simply by examining a car in a dream. Cars represent our personalities to which there are many facets. Sometimes we dream of tripping out in a sexy sportscar, but more often it is a sedate sedan. So pay attention to the type. It is not necessary to list lots of interpretations for the different shapes, brands and sizes because with a little common sense you will get the inference. Just one point though, and that is foreign makes indicate that you could be in a foreign environment.

Color usually has quite an importance since it indicates how flashy or unobtrusive you wish to be. The same can apply to the type of roof – convertible or enclosed sedan? Is it a two-seater or family car? Is it new,

ordinary, old, rusty, dirty, highly polished? Any of these factors can be applied to our personalities. The same applies to the ability of the engine to propel. Does it fire first time, is it in good order, is it always breaking down? Another feature is how often we change it. Are we chopping from car to car, in other words trying on different images, or do we stick with the current model until it falls to pieces? In fact, is it time we took it to the breaker's yard?

Having considered all these externals, who is driving it or is it stationary? Has it stopped for a good reason? If you are driving, it infers that you are taking an active part in your life. If you are a passenger be wary, especially if there is no driver. Try to ascertain who might be driving your personality. Are you constantly being pushed to one side or are you

happy to be driven? Could it be that you are a backseat driver, in which case, who have you let take the wheel, who do you want to run your life for you or are you just being bossy? Finally, is there a driver at all? Maybe you are not even in the car. It is simply parked or has been taken over by others.

With public transport we have given over the responsibility of our progress to others. This can be simply for our own convenience so does not have an immense significance, but on the other hand it shows that we allow the establishment to run our lives. Sometimes this keeps us in a rut preventing free expression. Or, of course, it could simply be keeping us on track, preventing us from going off the rails. Look for this when any kind of rail is involved – tram, train, monorail, trollybus.

Next, our progress needs to be

Far left: Going to extremes on the slippery slope. We should ensure we remain in control.

Top left : Personal effort is necessary, especially in a group environment.

Above: We should always remain in control and not be taken for a ride, nor be caught.

Below left: Our road is clear and protected, even so, it is a lonely road.

examined. Having passed up the responsibility, where are we being taken? Is it somewhere we want to go; are they in control of the situation; are we flowing freely or are we all snarled up; is the weather interfering; or is everything going swimmingly?

Examine the different types of propulsion. Firstly, we have our own two feet and the amount of effort we put in. Secondly, there are natural forces, namely wind with sails, wings, clouds, hurricanes, up and down currents, water with rapids and waves, snow with avalanches and ice, earth with landslides, earthquakes, eruptions and, gravity itself. Thirdly, we have animal power, either carrying us or pulling us and, finally, we have the man-made variety, the engine. And, of course, we can have combinations of these features. Understanding these is simple

Confronted by so many options, we must be sure to take the right route.

once we realize that on foot, we are responsible. With natural forces we are often at their mercy, no matter how clever we think we are, but we can harness them to a certain extent. The same applies to animal power but it is important here to realize there are two minds at work. With the last group, the man-made engines, we should be in control, but often we are not.

Direction is the next important point since it is taking us to our goals. Is the road ahead easy or filled with potholes? Can we see where we are going? Are we going off at a tangent or round in circles? We can understand how clearly this could relate to our lives.

Direction	Interpretation
forward	no problems
forward with	
stops	hesitation
backwards	backing off
retreating	retreating
sideways	going off at a tangent
to the left	using logic
to the right	using intuition
around	side-stepping
upwards	rising to higher levels/taking off
downwards	falling back/exploring lower levels
uphill	effort required
downhill	easy, but dangerous
upside-down	taking an alternate view/helplessness

circling	working round a problem/uncommitted/threatening
spiraling	moving upwards/dizziness
colliding	on a collision course
winding	taking your time
meandering	no clear direction
crossroads	a point of decision
maze	being lost/impenetrable barriers/going nowhere
labyrinth	caught in a rut/getting to the center of things
zigzag	proceeding with care/avoiding danger
topsy turvey	out of control
higgledy-piggledy	random dead-end

Left: Sometimes others need our guidance and we have to put effort into it.

Getting lost or taking the wrong connection is a regular theme. It is all about having no clear direction or persistently going the wrong way. It can be a cry for help, so pay good attention to it. A really common problem is that of missing the bus/train/connection, which is pointing out lost opportunities, missed up, have brake failure, come off the rails, become becalmed, get caught in a quicksand, fall down a hole, sink, take off with us? Again, this is very much about being in or out of control and is simple to interpret when you see the connection between the images and our journey through life. However, do not forget resent our current problems which inhibit our growth. The wall can be new indicating that our current barrier is new; old, showing the problem has been around for a long time; crumbling, indicating just that. There may be a way through, round or over, or it may be impenetrable. Maybe you feel you could just knock

We must put in a lot of personal effort to battle through our emotions, indicated by the water.

chances, overdoing things, and running out of time. Such dreams are encouraging us to open our eyes and stop throwing away all our chances. They can also suggest we stop worrying, since there will usually be another one along shortly.

The final consideration about journeys is impediments. How often does our transport malfunction – refuse to start, start and then stall, run out of fuel, breakdown, get a puncture, blow-up, steam-up, freeze-

that such a hold-up could have a beneficial effect. What about accidents? Are we on a collision course or is someone trying to collide with us? Have we been idle about keeping things in good repair?

Other hindrances are all the different types of barrier. In this category come walls, chasms, road blocks, barriers, gates, rivers, sea, fire, doors, guards, guard dogs, dead-ends: in fact, anything which gets in the way. A wall for example can rep-

it down anyway. On the other side is the future. If we can see over the wall, is there anything there? If nothing, then we have created nothing, if something how does it look? If you can't see over the wall it is because you are not yet ready to look, or you are maybe obsessed by your current difficulties.

Right: Here we are skimming over our emotions at high speed. We need to consider whether we are in control or avoiding the situation.

Chapter Seven

BUILDINGS

The next main feature in dreams is buildings which come in myriad shapes and sizes. We can divide them into several categories – places where we live, places of work, or places of worship.

We are all familiar with the "mansion of the soul" and this is what homes usually represent in our dream world. They are described as being the protective structures which we have built up around our-

selves since birth, so let's look at them at first, in that light.

There are all the types of house that can be found in towns and cities, ranging from elegant mansions to public housing, from regency terraces to slum terraces, from smart apartments to hovels and shacks, with all the immense variety of possibilities in between. These houses represent you in relationship with others, with a certain interdependency, yet being at the same

time, fairly self - contained, which is the epitome of city life. Country houses, however, present in two main ways. They are generally detached houses, either very well spaced out or quite closely huddled

Left: Concrete jungle, place of excitement, place of work or place of misery?

Below: Moveable houses like the houseboat indicate a rootlessness and also that one's personal structure is balanced on emotions.

together. The latter are found in villages, grouping together for the common good, while the others range from castles to country estates, from country houses to mudhuts and caves. Again, these environmental factors should be taken into consideration, even if the type of house resembles one in a town.

"I am fascinated by a low, thatched cottage which fills me with fear, although I recognize it. My mother gets sucked in. I feel relieved this happens to her not me, but then she is back and I get sucked in." The old cottage shows the problem is long seated, probably related to your youth because of its age and the presence of your mother. You obviously want your mother to take responsibility for your difficulties so you suck her in. However, this won't work, she is spewed up and you are forced to confront this situation.

Another type of home is the moveable one. Here we have caravans, mobile homes, houseboats, tepees, tents, igloos, straw houses. Each, in its own way, indicates a different attitude to living. They show a form of rootlessness, sometimes unavoidable, an unwillingness to be permanently tied.

Workplaces are buildings with more to do with our outside environment than our personalities. There are the dull, repetitive lives, usually of a manual type, shown by factories, quarries or mines, and workshops. There are the places of the white collar worker, offices and banks, where the work is mental, more to do with the logical side of the brain. There are the places of choice and exchange indicated by shops and department stores. There are the places of transit – airports, stations, ports and harbors, hotels, hospitals. There are the places of learning and/or stagnation – schools,

Left: The Taj Mahal, a place of peace and a lovers' tomb. The spires make contact with higher levels.

Below: The thatched cottage represents the cosy aspects of one's life, a desire for the past and the simple life.

universities, museums; places of entertainment such as theaters, cinemas, music halls, circuses, promenades, fun fairs – all of which indicate a facade, something that is not what it appears to be; and places of restriction like prisons.

"I was in a large department store. People were giving a man things to sell for them. I stood by the stand holding some cookies. The man picked one, ate it and said it was very nice. I was supposed to talk to him later but didn't." You are in a place of choice where you can sell your talents to improve your lot. However, your talents are nourishing others rather than you. You could change this but you decide not to bother.

Places of worship usually feature in more profound dreams since they are related to higher levels of ourselves. Churches and cathedrals tend to be the accumulation of all our spiritual beliefs. We are often in awe, and conscious of other beings or energies which touch us deeply. We usually experience extreme peace or drop into meditation.

Right: A place of peace and sanctuary.

Church towers and steeples indicate a need to contact higher levels of consciousness and if they are damaged they show neglect or an obsession with the mundane. Graveyards can be fearful places or show a need to contact things past.

"I was really upset and found myself in what appeared to be a church. There were a few people who ignored me. I climbed several flights of dusty stairs in the tower hoping to get a better view." You are afraid so you look for spiritual comfort. Because you are an unbeliever or a rare visitor, you are not greeted. Your spiritual levels are all dusty and little used.

Temples can be ancient, huge edifices or simple earthworks or clumps of trees. Here there is a much more ritualistic feel, often of expectancy. Also there can be a suggestion of sacrifice combined with sensations of power or powerlessness.

Is your building collapsing on you, in other words, is your world disintegrating around you.?

Your house should always have access upwards for ventilation and spiritual contact.

It is sensible to consider the overall atmosphere initially, both inside and outside, because this is often a strong impression. So, here are a few ideas. Do we feel at home, a stranger, comfortable, uncomfortable, wanted, unwanted, happy, sad, depressed, afraid, hot, warm, cold, neglected, rejected, or simply nothing at all?

Roofs are particularly important since they are our protections against the storms of life. If they are falling in, maybe things are about to crash in on us. If the roof is leaking, you are surrounded by irritations which are affecting you emotionally, something is getting in on you. You need to get up on the roof and attend to your upper aspirations. This is particularly important if you are involved in any occult matters or chakric workings. Chimneys are our routes through to the upper levels. Frequently, nowadays, they are unused, blocked, or missing all together. Thus the fire in our basements cannot survive since there is no draught to carry our energy skywards. Good ventilation is crucial.

Access to the dream house is important. How many obstacles did you encounter such as a winding, overgrown pathway, holes, trenches, obstructions, gates, barriers, fences, drawbridge, barbed wire, threatening people, or threatening animals. If these lead up to your house, why are you keeping the world at bay, not allowing it access to you? On the other hand, if you have been too accessible, maybe it is telling you to put up a few barriers. It can also be a clear demonstration of our limitations. The same applies to doors, shutters, curtains and windows. It is good to be welcoming and not shut

The kitchen, a place of nourishment, both spiritual and physical, can also represent starvation or frenetic activity.

yourself away, but sometimes we need to close and bolt them securely to avoid being so vulnerable.

"A friend calls me from an upstairs window and advises me to be careful about things. At my flat I am frightened to find the lock has disappeared. I look round but nothing has been taken." You are guided in your life from a higher level, if you pay attention. You appear to have a faulty lock, which shows inadequate protection. Take care.

"I returned home to find the door unlocked and people in the house. I told them to empty their pockets and leave." People are intruding into your life. Although you resent it you only show mild irritation. Instead of prosecuting, you let the burglars go free.

There is another aspect to doors, gates, and crossing all forms of barrier and that is of moving to another level of consciousness. Be aware of this. "I was led up some stairs into a magistrates court with people sitting at desks. Then we went through a wrought iron gate to the third floor. There were three balls which started to juggle." You are being led to

explore your own psyche, but when moving upwards, you should make clear judgements before progressing further. Thus you reach another threshold where things may have to be juggled for the right outcome.

The state of repair is the facade we present to the outside world. If our house is in immaculate condition, regularly painted and repaired, this is a good omen. Ruins speak for themselves. However, if it is dilapidated, in need of a coat of paint, with the doors and windows falling off their hinges, we need to look to our depression levels.

If you are outside, make a note of the details of what you see. For example, does the house have an open look – open curtains and windows, door ajar, and a welcoming garden? Is it in good repair, do the roof and chimmney give good protection? Alternatively, it can have a closed appearance – all doors and windows closed, shuttered, draped or curtained. The front door can be around the side of the house. Maybe there is no chimney – no connection to higher levels. Maybe the whole place needs repairing and decorating. All these descriptions represent us and how we present ourselves to the outside world.

The garage is where we keep the car, our personality (as opposed to our protection which is the house).

Is the car polished and beautiful, sitting in a nice clear garage because we love and appreciate it, or is it sitting muddily in the drive, with the garage filled up with all manner of dross?

The front door of the house leads us to a place of transition – the hall, which is the place between rooms. Whenever we find ourselves here in a dream, we know we are at a moment of choice. Coming in indicates we are leaving the world outside and can choose which room to enter. Going out shows a commitment, a decision made, to be taken out to the world.

The kitchen is often the first port of call. Kitchens are about nourishment on all levels, the need to nourish ourselves physically or spiritually, but equally to starve ourselves. Consider how this dream kitchen looks. Is it like Old Mother Hubbard's with empty cupboards, showing that it is time to go shopping? This could mean that your current life is sterile and you need to do something about it. On the other hand the dream could be about overeating, indicating that a few days fasting would be constructive. In both cases, lack of love is obvious. If the kitchen is full to overflowing again consider both sides of the coin. It could be that love is overflowing, that you have lots to give

Back doors are usually private entrances and lead to our secret gardens.

about nourishment, the garden is our secret and safe place. Although for some, it can be a hard, uninviting place, full of rubbish. We all have a "secret garden" in our lives. It is usually enclosed and accessible only to ourselves. No one can enter without invitation. It is a place for meditation and for retreat, where we can lick our wounds and recharge our batteries.

We need to consider the contents of the garden. If it is mainly vegetables then, like the kitchen, it is a place of sustenance. Is it excessively orderly and neat, or is it wild and overgrown? Both are reflections of your character. If it is overgrown, maybe you haven't visited it lately, so are neglecting the recharging process.

Basements and cellars are the places where we push all our unwanted things, particularly the unpleasant ones. Everything that we would prefer to forget or hide is hidden down there. Quite often in dreams as we approach the cellar, we are filled with dread. We truly don't want to confront all those moments of intense embarrassment, times when we cheated, stole, swore, lusted or lied. Those things that we definitely don't want the world to know about, We turn them into monsters, push them down and keep the door firmly locked. They are the stuff of nightmares and recurring dreams.

The dream mind won't allow us this luxury especially in our moments of weakness. Thus, when a vulnerable situation arises during our waking hours, the unconscious opens the cellar door in our sleep. The only way to empty the cellar of nasties is to confront them, acknowledge them and come to terms with them, realizing that honesty is the best cure.

However, as always, there is another aspect to basements and cellars. They are storage places for things of value such as coal and fuel to heat the house. There are often goods waiting to be recycled and many practical items are stored

and should start sharing. Or, it could mean that a time of fasting would be appropriate.

Kitchens are about food for thought, that you have reached a point in your life when you should consider things in more depth. They are also cosy, snug and safe places, where you don't have to put on a style. You can share the proverbial cup of tea. They are also quite creative places, as is any form of cook-

ing – places for expressing yourself without pretence. However, cleanliness should be examined. Could you be contaminating yourself or others. Is what you have to offer stale or going putrid? Are you sharing the soiled side of you? Are you offering poison?

Back doors are fairly private and away from the public eye, often leading directly from the kitchen into the garden. While the dream kitchen is

there. And, what about the wine! Sometimes they show the need to go within ourselves, to make contact with our innate wisdom, or even to hibernate for a while.

Living rooms are to do with our present circumstances, especially in relation to those around us. Special attention should be paid here to the general level of homeliness. Is the place inviting and lived in; is it excessively neat and tidy, or is it so untidy that walking across the floor resembles an assault course; is it covered with dust sheets? You can see how a simple image of a room can give you a clear indication of the state of your life

"I am in a big room of an old house, empty except for a fireplace and a big packing case. I feel there's a dead body in the case and it is my fault." The room is dominated by the packing case because this problem is so large in your life. It contains something which you thought was dead and buried long ago. It needs confronting so that you can come to terms with it and free yourself totally. The fireplace shows that you can get help from higher levels.

The dining room is slightly different from the kitchen in that it is about more formal nourishment, often on a grander scale. It could be to do with our need to create an impression for others. It is a place for assimilation, digestion and communication. On the other hand it can be cold and uninviting with such formality or sparsity that we feel rejected.

Although a study is normally a workplace, in the dream context it is worth considering the true meaning of the word which is to explore, learn and retain. This can apply equally to a library. However, in the latter it may be that you need to locate a particular book or even write your own.

"I dreamt I was in a library. A copy of Shakespeare's *Julius Caesar* fell

Stairways are places of transition between levels. Always be aware of what they are linking.

off the shelf." The dreamer did not understand this, so decided to read the play.   On questioning, he shrugged off the story.   However, when pressed to recall any part, he said he remembered the part where Brutus knifed Caesar in the back, but it didn't mean anything. When pressed again, he realized the point – that Caesar thought Brutus was his best friend, but he, too, had betrayed him. The dreamer suddenly registered shock.   He understood the dream. His best friend at work was about to stab him in the back.

Stairs, escalators and lifts can be about transition, but can also relate to our life's journey. In this context they indicate changing levels. They show whether we can safely make it up or down and offer opportunities to make contact with the deeper parts of ourselves. Be conscious of which parts of the house are being linked.

"I tried to climb some stone stairs which suddenly changed to descending stairs.   Walking down they changed and I was outside.   The stone steps were worn and had weeds growing through them. The stairs were like those in the illusion where you could go down or up indefinitely in a circle." Each time you think you have made it to a new level of achievement, you are back on the treadmill. You find yourself on the eternal circle. This is obviously a problem of long standing, shown by the weeds. The time has come to make the break.

"I find myself standing on top of a

large ladder. A friend at the bottom starts to shake it and ask me to come down. I ask him to stop but he ignores me. He has a sharp knife with which he has been peeling vegetables and has a bag of fresh celery. I wake up frightened." You have been working your way up the ladder of life and now find someone is shaking your foundations. Your friend is showing you that you need to cut away some of the dross and stop ignoring the basic necessities of life. You are afraid to descend to his level in case you lose your status.

Bathrooms are all about cleansing. They give us the possibility to examine the dirt and dross that we have accumulated on all levels of our being. By using imagery to externalize, we are enabled to wash the negativity away. The symbolism of Shakespeare's Lady Macbeth "Out damned spot! out, I say!" (Act V:1) is clear. She tries to wash away the spot of blood which represents her guilty conscience.

Finding yourself in a flood shows an emotional lack of control. Dripping taps indicate irritating persistence. Be conscious of the effort required to get clean and also whether you are washing yourself down the plug hole. Methods of washing can also carry some significance. Luxuriating in a bath can be quite different from taking a shower or having a quick wash. The temperature of the water can be relevant, too. Warm is not necessarily a pleasure and could occasionally indicate that we need warming up. A cold shower or a cooling bath usually have unpleasant associations unless you have got yourself into a hot spot and either you, or the situation, needs cooling.

"I was having a bath and through the door I saw my brothers running away from a large dinosaur. I wondered what to do, so hid under the bed." Bathing is washing your hands of a situation. Here, instead of fading away it is assuming very large proportions. Your brothers running away shows you will not get external support and beds are not good pro-

This is our place of cleansing and elimination of all the loads we are carrying.

tection from dinosaurs. You will have to confront the problem alone in the end.

Lavatories are about relieving ourselves, of releasing things that have been adequately processed and are no longer required. Urinating can simply be a physical need translated into the dream. However, it is also about letting go and, if we get the message the result is amazing. Just think of the relief of going after a long interval; it is frequently connected with stress and tension in our daily lives. Defecating is to do with eliminating unwanted memories or

experiences. Strangely, it is often associated with wealth, perhaps because it can also be interpreted as manure and "where there's muck, there's money."

"I dreamt that I was in the lavatory and that I was covered in excrement and couldn't find anything to clean myself. I went outside and every room was filled with the stuff. It was disgusting." It transpired the following day that, after protracted legal proceedings, our dreamer's divorce was finalized and she was to receive a very large settlement – more money than she had ever had in her life before.

"I am looking for a toilet. I eventually find one that is outside the cubicle with no privacy. I look for another toilet and find one that is even more public, set on a stage and very well lit." Loss of privacy shows some sort of threat and going to the toilet shows a need to relieve yourself of the burdens and problems of life. You recognize this but are not strong enough to act. Having the public light thrown on you is unbearable and you feel that everyone can see through you.

If you are locked out it can indicate that you are unable to release your problems. The same can apply when you can't find a toilet anywhere.

In the early part of our lives bedrooms are generally our place of secrets. The place where we could go and lock the door and do what we please. They are, therefore, to do with escapism, private indulgences and fantasies. Later in life we allow them to be invaded when we take a partner and then the sexual element comes in. If we are sharing a dream bedroom very careful note should be made of the other occupants.

"I dreamt that I was trying to make the bed after having made love to my husband but the base sheet was in small squares which I was trying to fit together so that certain marks would not show. I became aware that my mother-in-law was sitting in the corner of the room looking disapproving, wearing a baby's nappy and sucking her thumb." It transpired that this dreamer had real problems with her mother-in-law who disapproved of her as a wife for her son. She lived with them and quite clearly indicated to them that she thought sex was dirty and they were inhibited by the fear that she would hear them. She frequently resorted to childish and helpless behavior to get sympathy and to keep them apart.

Attics and lofts are storage places but usually on a more spiritual level, where we preserve our higher thoughts for future use. In the main, they are neglected places because so many of us nowadays have foregone the intuitional and inspirational in favor of the extreme material and mundane sides of life. So when we

arrive in the attic, it is covered with dust and cobwebs. It is important both to explore this area and to truly understand any objects that you unearth, and to clean the windows and let some light in.

"All the rooms are excessively messy. A friend appears and is really rude about the untidiness, especially on the upper floors, saying I obviously cannot manage on my own and I had better clean up. Then she offers to help me." The time has come to tidy up the rooms of life to make room for something new. Your friend gives you a warning to protect yourself in these new clean realms of experience. You should always take a guide and be pure in thought when going into the spirit world.

There are so many other possible rooms in our mansions that it is difficult to list them all. So from the interpretations above, we should be able, with a little thought to latch onto their meanings.

Bedrooms are our places of secrets where we can close the curtains. Beds can represent our sexual needs as well as rest.

Chapter Eight
PEOPLE IN DREAMS

People in dreams fall into a number of clearly defined categories. They are either actual people known to you, aspects of yourself, fictitious characters you recognize or just vague and unidentifiable. Initially, they can be taken at their face value, because your dream may be a literal one. More important, however, is what each character could represent, since dreams are about symbols rather than actualities. Fathers are generally about any form of authority. Spacemen are about alien influences. Royals are a desire for recognition. What we should be looking for is the archetypal energy behind the person.

According to Jung our personalities have certain distinct characteristics. Every human being, whether male or female, has both a feminine side, known as the anima, and a masculine side, known as the animus. Combined with this we have the self, or ego and the shadow.

In our waking lives, we clearly manifest our gender and it is left to the dream world to bring in the balancing effect. A weak, ineffectual woman who is obliged to take some positive action will often dream of a strong, efficient man indicating the need to develop that side of herself. Sometimes, there is a more subtle approach, where the dream man may appear incompetent but then through skill and mental agility, overcomes his adversaries. Here the

Left: Often our first view of the people around us.

Relationships are the most difficult things that we have to deal with in life.

woman is being shown that she needs to dig into her stronger feminine resources to find her answers. The same applies for men who may dream of women when they need to soften their approach and use more feminine wiles to get their own way.

The animus is the masculine, dominant and practical side of the female developed from her contact with the males in her family. She takes this image, this "man of her dreams" and tries to superimpose it on all future men that she meets. The same applies to the anima for the man, developed from his relationship with his mother and other females. How frequently do we come across the husband projecting his mother image onto the wife and vice versa?

"I was in a place I remember from my childhood and heard my brother

and father digging a trench. Then my brother was standing in the trench and my father was showing him a screen with an important picture on it." This shows the dreamer has been indoctrinated into taking on the masculine roles and being good buddies with other members of the team. This will result in her not only digging a hole for herself through association with these colleagues, but actually jumping into it. The showing of the screen indicates that it is time to look at the picture she is creating.

"A person called John needed help from my father who just ignored my request." You go to your father for help for the masculine part of yourself and are ignored. It clearly shows that you are expected to find the strength to take on this role yourself.

The ego tends to appear as the successful one, but frequently is only an observer, rather like you looking at yourself. The shadow represents those parts of ourselves that we refuse to confront. Tom Chetwynd in *A Dictionary for Dreamers* describes it as follows: "Think of the person you detest most in the world, mix in the worst characteristics of anyone else you know, and you have a fair idea of your own Shadow. It frequently appears in dreams in the image of people whom the dreamer dislikes or envies in waking life." It is our dark side and epitomizes our projections. I learned quite early on that the things I dislike most in other people are actually my own worst faults. It is not always ugly, it simply represents the other side of the coin.

"I was on a conveyor belt with others moving slowly towards a hole. It was being controlled by a gloating maniac. Gradually we all turned into liquid and flowed into a deep vat. I felt myself hitting the mass of thick, yellowy brown liquid. I thought: 'that's it, I'm gone.' I saw the maniac stirring the liquid around with a stick, looking crazed and delighted."

Left: Trapped by motherhood. The party girl has to stay at home.

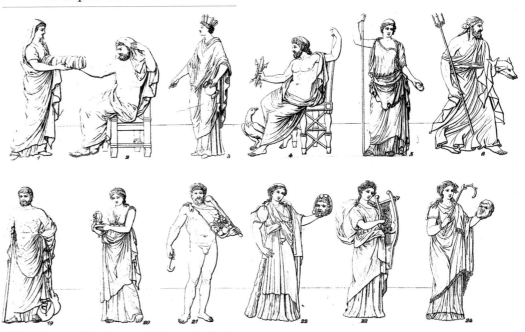
Which personality have we taken on today?

You are putting yourself back in the melting pot, undertaking a complete blend and change of form (like a brainwashing). The maniac is that part of yourself which is forcing this on you. It warns of your manipulating self and also that you are being sucked into the mass. What are you doing to yourself and those around you?

The first thing to consider is what aspect of ourselves does the dream person or persons represent. This is often difficult to identify so it is worth looking at the archetypal energies that they may represent. We are many-faceted and virtually all the characteristics mentioned below manifest within us at some time or another.

THE FEMININE

To many people the feminine is the epitome of the Goddess principle. What generally springs first into our minds is the wise old woman, the mother earth, our feminine connection with the source of all wisdom, the collective unconscious. She is the one we turn to in our greatest need, especially as the mediator between us and the supreme creative forces. The feminine principle manifests in terms of certain qualities. It is seen as wise, nurturing, ingenuous, receptive, intuitive, deep-thinking, sensitive, emotional, gen-

tle, feeling, caring, mysterious, virginal, flirtatious. We also see the obverse, the terrible mother, the earth that erupts around us, that disciplines us: rigid, domineering, possessive, narrow-minded, naive, weak, cold, hard, uncaring, sensual, erotic, bewitching, scheming, evil. It manifests in four main guises, each of which has two faces. We have talked of the anima which is pure femininity. The roles it plays are noted below.

The mother image usually brings to mind the Virgin Mary, a mother rocking her child to sleep or rubbing it better; a mother suckling her baby or preparing food in the kitchen, taking the children to school, doing all the chores, the shopping, the cleaning. All these images are about nurturing and caring and are gently protective.

However, the mother has another face. She can be excessively aggressive, especially in defense. She can be possessive, or pathetically demanding. She can be completely neglectful, self-absorbed and uncaring. She can refuse to break the ties and allow her chicks to fly. She devours. "I felt it would be safe to run past a woman sitting on the road ahead of me. I realize my mistake when I see she is holding a knife. I couldn't run back and had to keep going. She grabbed me and, half-crazed, wanted to kill me. I tried to reason with her but it made no difference." You are threatened by someone whom in normal circumstances would have protected you, but no amount of reasoning encourages her to see your point of view. You have probably invoked your mother's disapproval. It is also saying that it is wise to look before you leap.

So when we dream of a mother figure, first of all we need to ask ourselves what a mother means to us. Which of these categories does she fit into? What was our relationship with our own mother, or to the mothers of our friends? Do we need to be more caring or are we devouring, suffocating those around us? Female bosses and in-laws can come in this category. "A man I am attracted to

*Right: Nurturing, loving, protecting –
motherhood in its perfection.*

*Below right: The terrible mother who takes
away our freedom and seeks to devour us.*

*Below: The eternal wisdom of the planet
personified by the old woman.*

The maiden – young, unspoilt image of unsullied youthfulness.

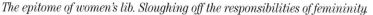

The epitome of women's lib. Sloughing off the responsibilities of femininity.

and I are in his mother's gothic style house on top of a steep hill. He is not very keen on me and the atmosphere is terrible." The fact that the house belongs to his mother and is at the top of a hill shows he still belongs to his mother or to his past associations and you have to struggle up to get near him. He is making absolutely no effort to come to you.

The maiden or the princess is the young, unspoilt image of unsullied youthfulness. She expresses lightness and happiness. She is the young heroine full of bright expectations who has not yet experienced the realities of adult life. She is still in the virginal state, but can also be the naive, unmarried mother.

Her other side is the streetwise youngster, the girl who is old before her time. Maybe she has had to look after her brothers and sisters. There is often a wildness about her. She is

found in the role of the seductress (Lolita), or prostitute, or the deliberately unmarried mother.

When you find this character in your dreamscape, look at that part of yourself, whatever your age. The maiden can appear in later life when we feel the need to re-experience these parts of ourselves. Are we yearning for that young, naive time when we were free from responsibilities, or refused to accept them and got away with it? Perhaps we are making our lives too complicated and need to get back to simple basics. We may need to cultivate these maid-like qualities. On the other hand are we being too naive; should we be drawing more on our maturity? For mothers, it can represent some aspect of their relationships with their daughters. Frequently, there is an unrecognized role reversal. Alternatively consider

work-mates, friends or simply fantasies or desires. Sisters, nieces, daughters-in-law, girl friends and colleagues fall into this category.

The mature woman is often seen in feminism. In her positive form, she is the bluestocking, the deep intellectual, frequently a spinster and often inward looking. She is the maiden aunt, the governess, the career woman dedicated to her work. She also appears as the mother whose children have grown and left, totally absorbed with herself, or doing good works to fill the gaps in her life. In the main there is an imbalance in this personality. The predominant features are a need to manage without men or to treat them as inferior beings.

Her other form is that of the huntress. She uses her intellect to entrap and, while dismissing men, uses all forms of seduction to gain

The masculine principle carrying all wisdom with him, unconcerned by evil and the passing of time.

mates come in this category.

The priestess or sorceress is the intuitional side of the feminine. These people seem capable of taking the overall objective view of a situation. They are very clear-thinking and unamenable to coercion or narrow-minded manipulation. They always seem to have the answers but you cannot lean on them because when you turn round, they are simply not there. There is a distinct feeling that they have contact with powers elsewhere since they invariably make all the right decisions. Frequently they either won't or can't rationalize.

The obverse here is the schemer, the woman who ever so casually destroys with a word, who drips poison in her gossip, damns with faint praise. She is the character assassin who finds fault wherever she goes always, of course, for the "best of reasons" and in the "nicest possible way." Surprisingly, she is often the "do gooder" since this role can be taken on for self-aggrandizement rather than altruism.

When these women appear in your dreams, try to see your motives really clearly. The definition is between objective action for overall good and manipulative action for self benefit. These females can be in any relationship with you.

THE MASCULINE PRINCIPLE

It is important to realize that the masculine is not the opposite of the feminine, but the complimentary part of the human species. Just as in the female, each aspect of the male has its obverse. The wise old man is the epitome of all the positive principles of the animus. He is god the father, the source of all cosmic wisdom and overall creator, the mentor. He is the character on whom we call and to whom we pray when in need, the external father principle, the ultimate adviser and protector. In his negative guise, he is the wrathful god, exacting penalties for misbehavior. He is without mercy. This is not interpreted as cruelty, however, but justified by his absolute authority.

her ends. She makes all the overtures. She is a dominant powerful personality who thinks nothing of trampling people under her foot and tossing them away when they have outlived their usefulness. She can also be seen in the woman who deliberately sets out to have affairs, with a sort of frenetic intensity. She can be described as "mutton dressed as lamb," i.e. the older woman pretending to be a teenager and unable to accept the ageing process. Usually, despite her reputation, men cannot resist her because in many ways she represents their latent need for a mother and the off-loading of responsibility, i.e. the woman in charge. They can take without concerning themselves with the consequences.

When this aspect appears in your dreams, you need to ask yourself if you are becoming too immersed in you work. Are you sharing enough, or have you become so absorbed that you are losing sight of a clear perspective leading to imbalance? Are there big gaps in your life? Alternatively, are you chasing the male simply for a one night stand and consequently avoiding any longterm commitments? Perhaps you feel over-stressed and foetal and would simply like to close your eyes and leave all the problem sorting to others. Aunts, older sisters, friends, in-laws, female bosses and work

The authoritarian father whose word is law.

The hero full of high ideals to help humanity.

In the main, the father represents the provider. He is the hunter-gatherer who preserves the race and procreates. His main roles in the family environment are those of authority, provision and protection. He also represents ideals and standards to live by and play to. We look up to him with respect and for approval. His other face is to be feared. This is the authoritarian character, the one who brooks no argument. He has no time for you or your opinions. He is frequently sadistic and uncaring, taking punishment and cruelty to extremes. He is the oppressive ogre, depriving us of individuality. He can also be the sex abuser.

So when the father appears in your dreams, recall which of the above describes your father. What is he actually representing for you? Either there is a trait in yourself that needs attention or else there is an external force infiltrating into your everyday actions. Is the authority benign or threatening? Fathers, uncles, older brothers, in-laws, bosses, dominating friends come in this category.

"My dad had bowel cancer and his insides were completely eaten away. He would not go to hospital and wanted me to be with him all the time." Your dad represents either your family or some other form of authority which is holding you back by playing on your sympathy. Cancer suggests that something is eating into the relationship, which is now an empty shell.

The hero is the young man with high ideals setting out on the quest of life. He is young, strong, idealistic and naive, fresh and untarnished. He is also the dreamer or poet, which can lead him to great achievements. He has great personal belief in himself, his ideas and his intention to change the world. As the lover he is more platonic than passionate.

His other aspect is the wastrel, the vagabond, the one who thinks the world owes him a living. Or he can appear as the hooligan, constantly disrupting the order of things. He has no desire to make any contribution and frequently, like Peter Pan,

Always look behind the face of the clown. It usually hides a sad and serious personality.

remains in eternal childhood and irresponsibility. He tends to live in prolonged procrastination and untidiness. Sex for him is a loveless form of physical gratification. Brothers, boyfriends, nephews, sons-in-law, work mates, and weak bosses come in this category.

The warrior is the mature man of experience who has suffered the knocks and bruises of life. He is worldly-wise, but on a mundane rather than spiritual level. He has considerable vitality and aggressiveness, being prepared to take on all comers. He can be very protective and possessive, absorbed with materialism and personal gain. He is frequently the teacher.

The villain, his opposite, has several guises. Firstly, the uncouth rogue who lives by his wits, or secondly a blunderer blindly trampling over all before him. Another face, however, is the sophisticated cheat or trickster who also makes negative use of his intellect. He often makes use of his maturity to dupe those younger and more innocent than he. Colleagues, uncles, brothers, nephews, in-laws are found in this category

Rather like the hermit, the high priest represents very high ideals and seems to obtain his wisdom from higher sources. He knows without logical reasoning. He shows the way through the tangled paths of life. He has a tendency to be ritualistic, yet quite objective and altruistic. He can be seen as the mentor, guru or personal guide.

Alternatively, the black magician is the megalomaniac. Everything he does is manipulated for personal gain only. He uses every means he can to achieve his own ends. He deliberately mesmerizes and uses innocence to pave his evil roads, regardless of the cost. He looks for followers to brainwash and form his power base. He is very subtle and frequently not recognized for what he is, having vampire-like tendencies. These can be people in any relationship to you.

The fool or jester is an interesting

The child can be innocence personified or intrinsically evil. . . Beware its face.

personality since it is generally a disguise. If we consider Shakespeare's conception of the fool we see that really he is the wise man, ("many a true word spoken in jest"). He uses laughter and joking to lighten heavy situations and atmospheres. In his "apparent" naivety he can "step in where angels fear to tread," virtually forcing others to look from a different angle. It is never wise to dismiss the fool without examination.

However, he does have another face, that of the real fool, constantly making a fool of himself. You will observe him in the eternal joker whose strenuous and artificial humor is tedious in the extreme. He

is not funny or even clever. This type of behavior is a cry for help, a desperate need for attention at any cost.

THE CHILD

The child in the main epitomizes innocence, inquisitiveness, absorption and growth. It is like an unwritten book or something malleable which can be shaped to the will and ideals of others. It is also like a sponge absorbing and being affected by whatever it comes in contact with. Out of this myriad of experiences, it grows and its very innocence has a wisdom about it which frequently seems to be well beyond its years.

Babies rarely represent human beings. They are normally creative talents or ideas to be developed.

The other face of the child is that of disruption and hyperactivity. On this level there is a lack of innocence which is replaced by a wily cunning. In fact, some children are distinctly evil. They are even quite sexually aware. They will deliberately stimulate without a clear understanding of the outcome. Much work can be done on the inner child which has frequently been abused mentally, physically, environmentally or morally, in fact, on all levels of its being. Very few of us have come through childhood unscathed by some alien form of negative indoctrination.

In dreams, babies usually have an entirely different meaning from the obvious. However, it is always wise to consider them literally first of all. Have you a need to return to the fetal; do you feel like a helpless baby? The more general interpretation is that they represent our ideas, our latent talents, our creations. Things that we have conceived and either do, or do not, give birth to or allow to develop. So often in our dreams, something terrible happens to the baby. We lose it, toss it out with the bath water, give it away. Each time, it means that we have neglected our abilities in some way.

"I am going somewhere on a bike with a small baby which is totally neglected and uncared for. I just about manage to feed it. The way is narrow, uphill and hard to find, but I am determined to get there." You have obviously been neglecting your talents while struggling up a hard and narrow route. What is being shown here is that your determination will win the day no matter how hard life may appear to be at present. The important thing is to continue to nurture your hopes.

There are other occasions when we feel that someone has stolen, or is about to steal, our ideas. This happens much more frequently than we realize, but it is not lost on the dream mind. This truly shows how valuable dreaming can be, since it can help us not to miss opportunities. "I was queuing at a supermarket checkout with a baby in the trolley. Two men were watching me and I knew they wanted the baby. They kept shuffling towards me and I had to keep moving other trolleys, which meant I missed my turn. Suddenly the baby was gone and I panicked. Then I saw it rolling towards me smiling. The men had not got it." Here you feel that someone around has an eye on one of your good ideas and would like to use it for their own ends. You are so concerned about protecting it that you are not developing it. However, now that you see what is happening, it comes back to you. The dream is telling you to act before someone else takes it from you.

"Two men in pioneer clothing paddled past me in a dug-out canoe containing a beautiful baby. Returning there was only one man with the baby, paddling strongly upstream against the current." The baby represents a creative idea being pioneered by people around you. You are apparently not involved closely, but are overseeing it. It will obviously be successful since the man is succeeding upstream, but it could be that he will need some help from you.

Dreams of pregnancy indicate that something is gestating. We have sown seeds or conceived and are now given the responsibility to bring things to fruition. An easy pregnancy augurs well, while a rough one shows either a reluctance or a lot of difficulties along the way.

Births speak for themselves and show that your idea has reached the light of day and now needs nurturing. Again, they can be easy or difficult. Stillbirths or abortions show that you have allowed your idea or talent to die, or decided to dispose of it before it has come to full term. They can also be miscarriages of justice or other actions. "I was at a station when suddenly a woman gave birth to two babies, the first was dark and looked straight at me, seeming to become older immediately whilst the other was tiny and had two faces." The two children represent ideas coming to fruition. The older one represents something you have had in mind for a long time so it is very well formed. The second is multi-faceted and gives the impression that it is slightly premature and needs more development from you to give it one clear identity.

"I am on a tandem with a pregnant woman. I felt this to be wrong because of lots of accidents on the road. Going down the hill I leaned over to one side knowing it would cause us to fall and possibly abort the child. We fell." The pregnancy shows you have a good idea conceived with others, but for some reason you want to sabotage it. Through your own actions, you cause the accident which could result in an abortion showing that you don't want to work further on the idea.

OTHER BEINGS
Since time immemorial angels in dreams have been messengers, and are well-recorded in the Bible. They can also be considered as your guardian angel or even your higher self. Their usual meaning is that of upliftment and links with higher levels of consciousness.

Most of the well-known angels are archangels and some are recognizable. Raphael is connected with the east, with spring, with dawn, with air and the sylphs, and with communication. He is usually seen dressed in a yellow cloak, a hat with a wide brim, and winged sandals, carrying a fish and staff. Michael represents the south, summer, midday, fire and the salamanders, and creativity. Michael has golden hair and wears a gold cloak and robe and usually carries a great sword with which he slayed the dragon. Gabriel is found in the west, with autumn, evening, with water and the ondines and with emotions. He sometimes carries the great horn of visions and glad tidings and occasionally seven white lilies.

He has white hair and is dressed in silver, having lunar connections. Uriel is found in the north, with winter, midnight, with earth and the gnomes, and with stability. He is the giver of wisdom and is seen against a dark, starlit sky. If they appear in your dreams, listen to what they have to say and also look for the underlying messages from their associations.

Aliens frequently appear in dreams nowadays and usually indicate that one is straying into unfamiliar territory, where things are strange and unrecognizable. They

What you gestate, give birth to or abort are those talents that need the light of day.

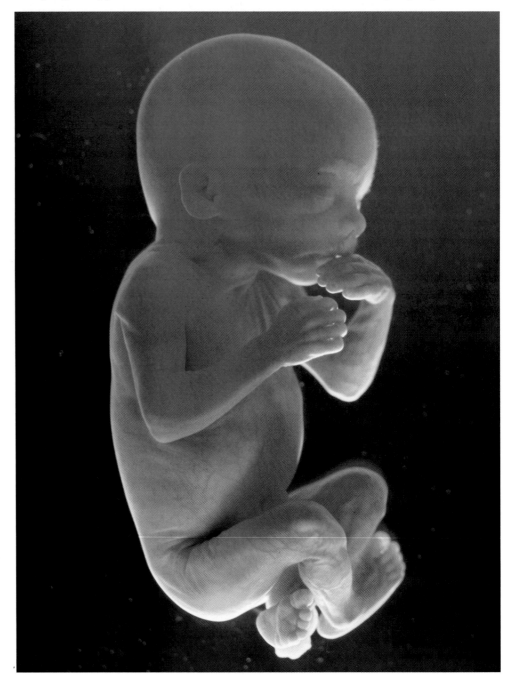

can also be guides bringing messages from apparently external levels of consciousness. Generally, however, they should be treated like foreigners, indicating that we need to learn their language and tread carefully rather than be dismissive.

Gods and goddesses are extremely symbolic since this is the original purpose for their being at all. Human nature needed names for certain energies and types of experience and so created anthropomorphic images to explain and share with others. Examining the many pantheons that exist world wide will show the parallels. Each has its father, mother and son, its shadow, its scryer, its oracle, its mystic, its priest, its healer etc. Each represents an aspect of archetypal energy.

Royalty and celebrities are common in dreams and usually indicate a need for fame or recognition, being accepted by them. Being in the presence of such people also emphasizes one's own insignificance. It is well to realize, however, that theatrical people are not what they seem. They are playing a part and can be presenting a false image. Which part are you actually playing? In Britain, dreams about entertaining the queen to tea are very common.

Ancestors usually indicate a need to look into our past for answers. We are all the culmination of the lifetimes of many generations and through our genes (DNA) which are constantly passed on, we may have access to all the experiences of those who lived before us. It is quite a remarkable thought. This enables us to have far memory dreams and to explore past life regressions. Thus dreaming of ancestors or grandparents means we are being asked to look backwards and draw on the past to help with today's problems.

Ghosts are apparitions which haunt and this is the clue. They represent something that we are unable to let go of. They hang around, appearing each time a pattern is repeated, like visiting a haunted room. They are also things which we can see right through, in a similar

Angels are the messengers from other levels of consciousness.

way to veils and illusions. Understanding their source helps to release them. We can also hold onto the spirits of those who have died by our excessive grieving, forging strong chains of guilt and worry for the migrating soul. Dreams help us to recognize this and sever the links.

"Every year since his death, I dream my father comes to life and knocks on the door. Nothing else happens and each year I cannot rest properly until those dates have passed. I was very close to my father." Deep down you wish your father was still alive and are holding on. Because of our love we cling on and don't allow our loved ones to pass on. Your father appears each year to ask you to release him. Give him permission to move on and the dreams will cease.

Very occasionally, ghosts are sent to us from an outside thought from one who is thinking constantly about us. These hauntings are not necessarily negative or evil, just uncomfortable. The simple way to deal

with them is to ask quietly and firmly that they return whence they came. "The bedclothes were being pulled off me by a woman ghost. She had her hands very close around my throat." Someone somewhere wants to remove your protections and to silence you. It is important to identify who may be threatening you in this way. Imagine you are protected within a shining bubble when you go to sleep so that unwanted thoughts will be mirrored back to the sender.

"I awoke suddenly to feel Keith standing by my bed looking intently at me. When I opened my eyes, there was no one visibly there, but I could still feel his presence. During the previous day, I knew he had a very strong interest in me but had given the matter no further thought." This could be a wish fulfilment dream but also Keith could have been linking in with you with great intensity and you picked it up. This often happens with intense emotions, particularly between mothers and children and where there is sexual attraction.

Chapter Nine

ANIMALS, BIRDS AND AQUATICS

From time immemorial mankind has been using animals as metaphors for human behavior. We are also animals and express similar habits and instincts, and they can be said to represent the instinctual sides of us. Herding and flocking are easy to recognize in the human. People tend to cling together for the security of the group, to participate in activities because everyone else is doing them. Rather than stick out like a sore thumb we want to match and blend. We succumb like animals to the pecking order. We know our places in the hierarchy and when we overstep and throw our weight around, we are cuffed back into place like any other young pups.

In dreams, animals can be aspects of ourselves or represent emotions, fears or possibilities. Take for example a dream about walking a dog. If the dog is in charge and pulling like mad on the leash, it shows that either we are being dragged through

Right: Dogs usually represent our friends and can display clear characteristics. They also guard the Underworld.

Left: The king of the jungle is proud and strong but also given to vanity.

Tigers are powerful and secretive. They represent stealth, power, cruelty and strength.

life by our friends, or that we are being held back from our rightful roles. Wild animals and birds indicate a sense of freedom, but also untamed instincts. They can be a warning that we need more discipline to live within our self-imposed civilization. Domesticated animals, on the other hand, show amenability, or a preparedness to work for the common good. Caged or penned animals fall somewhere between the two, since some were once wild, while others have been bred in captivity. Pets show a caring side to our natures but alternatively a patronizing aspect, too.

Animals are part of the shape-shifting skills of the Shaman on the inner planes. He usually has his own particular animal guide who protects and leads him and stays with him through thick and thin. At other times his spirit can take on the energy of a particular animal, using its instinctual features to alleviate a difficult situation. An example of

Cats represent our intuitive side. They are also sexy and promiscuous with a great propensity for survival.

this comes from a friend of mine who dreamt that she was being attacked unfairly by a friend at work. Because the dream was lucid, she changed herself into a tiger and frightened her tormentor. After that she had little further trouble at work.

Everything we do to and for animals represents how we are treating ourselves or those around us. They are self-explanatory. Take for example, bridles, halters, reins, saddles, collars, leads and lead reins, chains, hobbles, nose rings; caging, penning, herding, trapping, hunting; bathing, brushing, feeding, shearing, branding, nursing, whipping. Many of these words are used as metaphors in our everyday language.

ANIMALS

Dogs appear frequently in dreams and the most common meaning is that they are your friends. This comes from their characteristics of loyalty and protection. The different breeds of dog will all have meanings according to our encounters with them in our waking lives. They can also be guide dogs on the inner as well as the outer planes. The large black dog can represent the jackal-headed Egyptian god, Anubis, the guardian of the gateway to the Underworld. He can also be helpful in finding lost items. Sometimes, however, they attack and bite. This could represent your animal nature or friends who should be caring, turning aggressive. Also consider the dog-in-the-manger (awkward or stubborn behavior) which is much more common than realized. Do not forget the hounds of heaven, who will hunt without mercy. They will root out secrets however deeply hidden. Even though we hate to admit it, this can be an act of friendship.

Cats are connected with our intuitive selves and ability to survive the nine lives. They are much more aloof than dogs, tending to make use of us rather than be truly friendly. They hunt during the night which gives them a bad reputation. They are also considered sexy and promiscuous. They are one of the few creatures that play with their victims before killing them. They spit and scratch. They have been part of human households as far back as records go. They have been worshipped and revered but also appear as the familiar of witches. The pure black cat is thought to be lucky. With so many differing characteristics, we need to assess them most carefully in our dream symbology.

Lions and tigers have many of the same characteristics as cats and represent a wild and more expansive aspect. Lions, the kings of the jungle, have power and nobility which will test us. They appear in all cultures with similar meanings, where they are equated with the sun and solar energy. They appear in heraldry rep-

Animals – including sheep – and the characteristics they represent play a large role in dreams.

resenting the masculine, the solar, the positive part of a duality. Tigers are more about power and stealth, cruelty and strength. Riding a tiger means danger and a paper tiger is a person who appears fierce but is in fact, weak and ineffectual.

Horses represent personal driving forces within us and show whether we are masters of them, a form of individual horse power. So often we find them out of control, running away with us or refusing to function. Horses can also be a means of escape. They are proud and willing, and possessed of great speed and power. They are also thought to be messengers between the earthly climes and the spiritual. Some schools of thought see the rider as the higher self and the horse as the lower self, which is interesting sym-

bolism since it covers the aspect of two minds, with one knowing better than the other how we should run our lives. It is a comfortable image for spiritual guidance since the horse is considered to be a noble animal. We should think of all the colloquial expressions connected with horses as well, such as "being on a high horse" or "looking a gift horse in the mouth."

In our present cultures pigs, swine and wild boar represent greed, gluttony, filth, and all that is ugly and stupid. Pigs embody bad manners and ignorance. They show everything that is gross in nature. Pork is also a forbidden food in some religions. The wild boar evokes uncontrolled sexual needs. This reputation is unfair, as when allowed free range, pigs are remarkably clean and

Top: Horses are our driving force and how we control it.

Above: The pig and the boar epitomise gluttony, filth and stupidity. However, they are also a source of great wisdom.

Right: Bulls represent aggression and bluster together with strength and stability.

caring. In the past they were symbols of fertility and great wisdom. They were also equated with the Terrible and Devouring Mother since they were capable of destroying their litters. "Casting pearls before swine" is an expression to consider.

Snakes and serpents are truly archetypal symbols and should be considered either as sexual images, or as representations of evil and temptation. This is because most people are afraid of them and we need to examine strong first reactions. They also indicate deceit and writhing and wriggling to avoid capture or ruthless ambition. They are at home above the ground in trees, on the ground, under the ground and in water, which shows they are difficult to avoid.

Snakes also have a more profound meaning, that of lower energies rising to spiritual heights, the Kundalini. They are symbols of creativity, mysticism and healing. By raising these energies correctly the body is brought into balance and attains enlightenment. This is the meaning behind the caduceus which in various forms is used as an emblem of healing today. One can also be a "snake in the grass" or be as "wise as serpents".

The bear is a powerful symbol. It is one of the sacred animals associated with Artor, the north and the element of earth. We are so used to the image of teddy bears that we can completely overlook its natural characteristics. It is immensely strong, powerful and can be dangerous. Woe betide those who feel it is cuddly. Bears are also known for their bad temper and were often maltreated as exhibition items in the past. For some cultures the bear is revered and represents their entire sustenance; they ask permission of the bear's higher self before killing it. It has a protective, motherly image. It is associated with winter, retreat, resting and hibernation.

The stag is renowned for its strength, endurance, its sexual prowess and control of the females. It is solar and one of the sacred ani-

Above: We all know the teddy bear but archetypally the bear represents strength and the principle of hibernation and rest.

mals of the European culture associated with Cerunnos, the east and the element of air. It is frequently solitary which can represent bachelorhood.

Bulls and cows are both sacred animals, and sometimes connected with the mythical Minotaur. For many centuries there were bull cults throughout the world, the most famous being that of the Minoans. Bulls are famous for their aggression and blustering. It has an earthy stability and stolidness. The cow is known as Mona, the sacred cow and is connected with the west and element of water. In India cows are revered and cannot be killed or

Above: The stag is again about strength coupled with sexual prowess. It also indicates the bachelor.

Above: Monkeys often indicate the trickster because they are mischievous and eternally restless.

Left: The symbol of thoughts emerging from the depths. It can also move laterally in tricky situations.

spring, viz the mad March hare.

The monkey represents all that is infantile, mischievous and naive. It is a form of repression. It is often shown as the trickster and is difficult to take seriously. It has a tendency to take and use the ideas of others.

AQUATICS

Aquatics include animals that live on land and in water, together with creatures, such as fish or lobsters, which live permanently in water. Because of their watery connections, they are invariably related to the emotions or things surfacing or emerging from the deep unconscious. So, if we dream of fish, something is stirring and trying to

eaten. Cows tend to be passive, motherly and nurturing.

Rabbits are symbols of fertility and fast multiplication. They are also gentle, but very timid, and often the only sight one gets of them is their bouncing white tails. Rabbits look cute, but can also be incredibly

destructive, getting into places where they are not welcome and eating fresh young shoots. They should not be confused with hares which can run at speed over great distances and are connected with the moon. Hares are the original Easter bunnies and can represent the beginning of

attract our attention, which can be slippery or elusive or even fishy.

Salmon are thought to be the original sentient life form. They are symbols of wisdom from the distant past when they were sacred, especially with the Celts and the North American Indians. Eating salmon was supposed to produce infinite knowledge. The pattern of its life cycle shows the ability to travel great distances and keep the memory codes over long periods of time to return to the exact source.

Dolphins are an important symbol for many people today. The dolphin represents a transition from the sea to the land coupled with remarkable intelligence. It indicates fun, happiness, good company, and spiritual enlightenment. When it appears in dreams it has a powerful message.

Lobster and crabs often come up in dreams from the depths of the deep unconscious. Crustaceans are more primitive forms of life, and represent our unformed ideas and energies. The crab progresses sideways and can mean avoiding something or lateral thinking. It can also indicate a crabby nature.

The crocodile is usually a warning about danger. It is well disguised and emerges unexpectedly, revealing underlying trouble. It is also about deceit, falsity and hypocrisy. Crocodiles shed tears over their victims as they devour them, hence the phrase "crocodile tears". It is an example of false sympathy.

CREATURES OF THE AIR

Birds can be gregarious or solitary. They represent flocking and migratory instincts, with an ability to travel great distances. They are the messengers. Alternatively, they are the watchers. They take an overview, being able to observe from considerable heights, the tops of trees or buildings as well as the air. The following old rhyme expresses this rather well:

Right: The eternal symbol of peace. It can be sent out to explore unknown horizons.

Below: Dolphins are always powerful dream messengers bridging the two levels of consciousness.

A wise old owl sat on an oak
The more he saw, the less he spoke
The less he spoke, the more he heard
Wasn't he a wise old bird?

The eagle and the hawk are sacred in many cultures. The eagle is considered to be the messenger direct

Above: The wise old owl represented wisdom since time immemorial. It also hunts silently and at night.

Right: Butterflies are about transformation through a number of stages. Always consider which you are at.

Left: The eagle is about taking an overview, the ability to rise above problems. They are sacred to many cultures.

from god since it is able to look directly at the sun, fly to great heights and to be far seeing. It is very important in North America as a national emblem which represents these qualities. It also represents ambitious high-flying aims, leading to dominance. The hawk, on the other hand, is more deadly. It has much sharper eyesight for its prey and swoops with remarkable accuracy. It can be captured and partially trained to work for man.

The dove is the eternal symbol of hope, love and peace, also simplicity and freedom.

The owl has always been associat-

ed with wisdom as shown in the poem above. This is probably because of its ability to see in the dark and its almost silent flight which enables it to move undetected. It is connected with the Mother Goddess, and it is also a predator.

Bugs and insects usually represent irritations since they cause nuisance and frequently bite or sting. They

can also be an essential part of the food chain and be important for keeping other nuisances under control. Some lead extremely well-organized and ordered lives.

The butterfly is definitely about transformation because of its life cycle. In dreams it is about the final outcome of some earlier sown seeds/larvae which go through a

Above: The satyrs of the woods haunt our mythology and we still retain the fear of the green man and his cohorts.

Left: The centaur is the combination of man's intellect and his instinctual or more bestial nature.

ed to explain the unexplainable. In a number of cultures animals are combined with humans to create a blend of different characteristics.

Monsters are creatures invented by us to deal with our fears. They can take any shape or form, but are often related to our earlier experiences with myth and fairy tale and now, probably television and film. They clearly indicate a refusal to face up to our terrors in waking life. They can be identified by their major characteristics of action and emotion.

The centaur is a combination of man and horse. Thus we have the intelligence and skills of the man superimposed on the speed and

number of major changes to achieve the needed results. Thus it tells of waiting and watching.

MYTHICAL BEASTS
These are figments of the human imagination which have been invent-

The dragon is the archetypal energy that stimulates all things. It is the destiny of man to learn to control it.

drive of the horse. The lower instinctual side is manipulated by the intellectual.

The dragon appears in myths all over the world and is thought to be a flying version of the serpent. Some see it as epitomizing good and others evil. It can represent the life force and sexual energies, while at the same time having the purifying and transformational qualities of fire. It can also represent deep inner fears,

and the slaying of a dragon is extremely powerful. They frequently guard treasures, so dealing with them in the dream world can bring about great release and discovery of things you did not know you possessed.

The phoenix is about transformation and rebirth as it rises up out of the ashes. Sometimes we need to symbolically destroy all of our present circumstances and metamorphosize the remains into something

fresh and new.

The unicorn is one of the most famous of the mythical beasts and usually represents purity, virginity and altruism, although for some it is phallic and symbolizes sexuality. It can be both aggressive and gentle. Its horn was thought to be a water diviner at one time with the ability to detect and extract poison. It is a lunar image and appears in heraldry as the polarity to the lion.

Chapter Ten

ENVIRONMENT

All of life is cyclical and it is remarkable how important a part time plays in our dreams. We need, therefore, to explore the correspondences since they can have very powerful associations. Most dreams tend to take place in the present or in no apparent time phase. However, any dream that goes back in time relates to our past experience. If we dream of childhood, of grandparents, of ancestors, we need to examine the facts within the context of the past. In a similar way, dreams which appear to relate to the future or space travel could fall into the realm of pre-cognitive.

Day and night, dawn and dusk, midnight and high noon, each have a profound significance. We have built-in reactions for each period of the day. There is the expected behavior combined with our individual behavior. The early morning waker – the lark, is a very different body from the owl who stays up late at night. Their dreams can have considerably different interpretations.

The same applies to the seasons of the year. Spring is a time of stirring and awakening and equates with childhood; summer a time of attraction and luxuriant growth, equating with youth; autumn is the time of

Right: Despite our technological world we cannot avoid the cycles of Nature.

Left: The technological environment is overtaking us all, introducing new symbology into the dream world.

In villages and surrounding farms people relate more personally to one another.

fruition, of harvest connected with maturity; while winter is the time of retreat and rest and old age. These festivals have been celebrated for thousands of years and are centered on the cycles of the sun: the solstices (December and June), the equinoxes (March and September), and the intermediate quarters of the elements – Imbolc (February) is the beginning of spring, Beltane (May) is the beginning of summer, Lughnasa (August) is the time of harvest, and Samhain (November) is the begin-

ning of winter. Each of these festivals has its pattern of human behavior and helps us to understand where we are on our pathway through life. In the dream world recognizing these natural time scales can help tremendously with pacing ourselves in our waking lives.

We can also take into account the weather patterns around the time cycles. If it is obviously high summer and we are in a snow storm, the life situation could be quite tricky. In the same way, intense heat in the

resting time of winter can lead to unnatural growth. These somewhat bizarre images can tell us a lot about ourselves. Different types of weather – calm, cloudy, hot, cold, gloomy, threatening, stormy, foggy, etc. – can mirror, through association, what is currently happening in our lives and what to be wary of.

THE ENVIRONMENT
Where your dreams take place and the dominant features around you are quite significant depending on

Above: When we find ourselves in a prison cell we need to look to our waking life and try to recognize the bars.

Below: The cycles of time influence us and divide our lives into regulated packages.

their emphasis. Inside can be protective, cozy, safe, or a trap, while outside indicates freedom, lack of control or exposure.

Anything with a historical connection shows a need to examine your own past or else to understand the significance of the century in question. Foreign countries usually mean an alien or unknown environment where you can possibly get lost. Theaters, films, television or circuses usually show that all is not what it seems to be. There is play-

acting going on.

Ports, harbors, airports, stations, bus stops etc. are all places of transit and indicate that you are passing through or making connections. In almost all of these incidences, an outside agency is usually involved so we are not always totally in control.

Towns, cities and concrete jungles, industrial sites, and parks are all to do with group energy where people mass together impersonally, usually for material gain rather than social interchange. In villages, farms and estates, on the other hand, people are more interdependent and relate more personally to one another.

Jails, cells, prison camps, schools, monasteries, mental institutions, cellars, caves, tunnels can all be connected with a loss of freedom. Battlefields and war zones speak for

Above: Dreaming of wars clearly shows there is conflict in your waking life.

Left: A frozen landscape shows something is stuck in our lives The problem is difficult if there is a mountain to climb.

Below: Beaches are about manifesting from water onto land, important places of change.

Above: Bridges are about making links between people or situations.

Right: We all know about the secret garden, our place of retreat and security.

themselves, so beware.

"I am floating over a high plateau. Beneath me there is a war going on with very modern weapons, but the men are dressed as Romans. I was told it was 1540. I said it couldn't be because these weapons were not invented. Being chased, I float away down a red mountain." There is a powerful aggression in you. You want to fight with modern weapons, but feel you only have more primitive equipment. The red mountain also represents your anger and you are trying to fly above the situation without truly participating in it.

Bridges are about making links. They can join together compatible or conflicting elements in our lives. Remember what they are spanning. It can be deep and dangerous or

comparatively harmless spaces. Cliff tops, precipices or window ledges are major warnings. There is the fear of failure or of falling or that you are on the edge of something, which need not necessarily be bad.

Gardens have a particular meaning. They are frequently enclosed, and sometimes hidden, the secret garden. These are our special places of retreat where no one can get at us. Quite often we have a resident mentor who really cares about us and gives wise advice (see Chapter 7). Caves often have a similar interpretation unless they are cold and wet. Being in one is like going back to the womb.

Above: Water relates to our emotions, sensuality, sexuality and the deep unconscious mind.

Left: Something has invaded your secret garden.

"I am in a garden full of daisies leaning ominously towards me. I feel like running away but I can't because the daisies will attack me if I try to move." You have allowed your secret place, your deepest secrets, to be invaded. Daisies usually mean purity and innocence and here they are being used against you by someone unscrupulous.

THE ELEMENTS

It is important to be aware of an elemental dominance in your dream of water, earth, air, or fire, and also to consider whether you are receiving and reacting, or giving or dominating.

Water relates to our emotions, sensuality and sexuality and the deep unconscious mind. It can be expansive and calm, cold and forbidding, muddy and unpleasant, slimy, hot, flowing, or ice-bound to men-

Beware of the power of water lest it overwhelm you.

tion a few ideas. You may want to throw off your clothes and bathe in it, dabble your hands in it, paddle, or go nowhere near it. You may have a lake, a pool, a river, a trough, a puddle, a bucket, a sink, in fact any sort of spot for the accumulation of water.

So if your dream contains rivers, lakes, oceans, swamps, marshes, quicksands, floods, tidal waves, beaches, or ice, you can be sure that something profound is going on for you. The condition of the water helps to give you clues to the state of your emotions, e.g. stormy, muddy, fast-moving, sluggish, still, clear, windswept, frozen. If something is crawling out of the water or emerging from the very depths, then something on an emotional level is surfacing that has been repressed. The greater the depth, the longer the repression and the greater the

release. "I am standing by a small powerful river with a bridge over it which I am apprehensive about crossing. On the left the flow is intense and on the right there is a sheer drop. Suddenly there is a great torrent which takes a wall with it. Then everything is peaceful and the remains of the wall offer a safe passage over the water." There are strong emotions here which need to be released before the gap in your relationships can be safely bridged.

You need to allow the flood to take place and things will be destroyed in the process. However, your foundations are sound and peace awaits you.

Beaches are interesting since they are a combination of land and sea (earth/water). They are, therefore, transitional places where our slates are washed clean and we can make a fresh start. Tidal waves rarely drown us but rather, show that we will survive immense emotional upheavals.

Above: Man is composed of all the elements and any one dominating creates an imbalance.

Left: From the earth the seed grows and when nurtured can reach the very heavens.

Pools or bowls of water have profound meanings, firstly because they are usually still and we can often see the bottom and what, if anything, is rising and secondly, because they mirror or reflect. Wells and oases are interesting because they indicate refreshment when in need. However, they can also represent pollution, entrapment or stagnant situations.

The Earth frequently dominates and is to do with stability and strength. It is shown in countryside containing mountains, valleys, fields, hills, moors, tundra, steppes, plains, woodland, deserts and jungle.

Again, notice how are they presented. Is your dreamscape bleak, cold, deserted, warm, inviting, a struggle to get through, cultivated, or rich? Are you constantly going uphill — having a tough time; downhill — slithering on the slippery slope; hidden from the sun or being roasted; caught in an earthquake? The earth element gives clear indications of our security. "I was in a jungle and seemed to be flying just above the ground which seemed to be marshy." From this dream it would seem that your life has been rather like a jungle recently. The fact that you are flying shows you are now releasing yourself from what has been impenetrable and holding you back.

Meadows or fields show where you are in life at present. If it slopes to the left it indicates a leaning to the logical; if it rises to the left, you may have difficulty with the logical side

Above: Dreaming of a desert shows a bleakness in your life, however, it is also about surviving inhospitable conditions.

Right: If we put a lot of effort into cultivating the earth we will be well rewarded.

of life. If it slopes to the right, you tend to work in the intuitional and, similarly if it rises, you have difficulty with this.

Pathways represent your current progress. If straight, you know where you are going and are getting on with life. If it meanders, then that is where you are just now. If it slopes up then life is creating difficulties or hardships and, if it slopes downwards, take care! If it goes around the perimeter, that is how you are progressing at present, taking the long way round.

Air is more difficult to define

because we can only see, feel and hear its effects. We cannot see it for itself. In the main, we associate it with the sky and clouds. It is connected with communication, so all the various effects that it has on its surroundings relate to how we are putting ourselves across. This can be anything from a zephyr or breeze, to a full-blown hurricane or tornado. Be aware of how it feels and the sound it makes, it could be telling you something really important. Messages are carried on the wind. How do we sound on the air?

"I returned to my father's windmill in Poland. Inside there were several men sitting near the walls." The windmill indicates the element of air. The men represent the elders, the source of wisdom. Here you need to recall things learnt in your youth and communicate them in the present.

Finally, fire manifests in a myriad of ways and relates to creativity and transformation. Whatever is touched by fire has its form changed. It can

Left: The element of air is invisible. We can only see its effects yet it can be harnessed to our benefit.

Above: Fire, the great transformer, nothing that it touches can ever remain the same.

never be the same again, like the phoenix out of the ashes. In the landscape it shows in deserts, volcanoes, forest fires, bonfires, beacons, campfires, or burning buildings, while in the home we have hearth fires, central heating, electricity, gas, electric blankets and other appliances, candles, and matches. Its energy can vary from gentle control and warmth to smoking, smoldering, erupting, raging or exploding. When fire appears in your dreams, be conscious of extra energy or of change.

"I went into a flower shop and bought a flower arrangement with a lace-covered baby's crib in it. Suddenly the crib burst into flames and the shop assistant said it was the wrong time of the year to light it. The baby died." Flowers are to do with hope and promises for the future, so the baby (your creation) should develop into something important. However, it needs first the transformation of fire before it can grow.

Chapter Eleven

THE HUMAN BEING

The human body is probably our greatest and most used symbol, each part of it representing some emotional trauma. The simple way to understand it is to take each part in turn with its several meanings to which we can add our own personal ones. See how each body part is represented and interpret this association. Look for puns.

Hair   Hair indicates strength and a cover for your thoughts and ideas. How is it shown? Cut or balding means losing strength or protection. Tangled shows confusion, plaited an orderly situation etc.

Head   Is to do with the mind, analysis, getting ahead, being a head (or leader).

Ears   To do with hearing or deafness.

Face   Our appearances or recognition of others. Facelessness can be fearful but also can indicate our special guides. Consider, too "facing up to things."

Eyes   To do with seeing, blindness or the mote in your eye. They are the windows of the soul, so one needs to look under the surface. There is also the third eye or single eye, the source of intuition. Spectacles

Left: Man and woman's greatest problem, finding their individual identities.

Right: It's not the image but what's behind it.

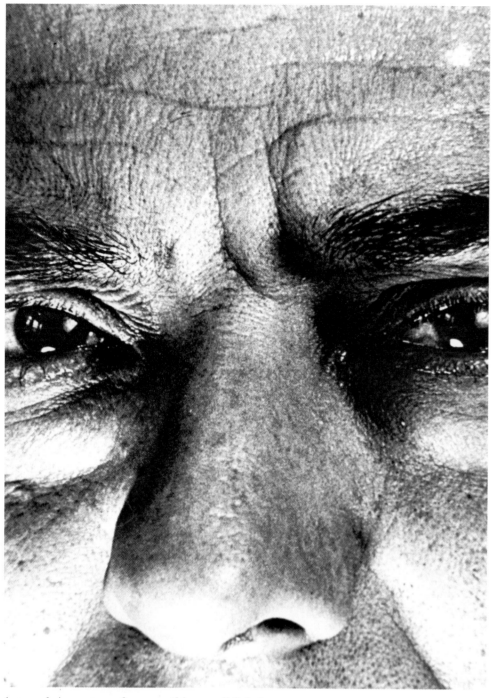

Are you being nosy or does something smell fishy?

Is there something you can't handle, or have you been too open handed?

also come into this category.

Nose   To do with smelling, loss of smell or something "getting up your nose." Also nosiness, inquisitiveness and knowingness.

Mouth To do with taste, with silence or talking too much. Paying lip service or stiff upper lip.

Teeth   Are about biting, chewing or grinding or something getting stuck in your teeth. They are also about maturity – losing baby teeth and growing seconds; wisdom, when these teeth are in question; talking too much and giving away secrets or old age when the teeth are falling out.

Neck   Supports the head or can be a "pain in the neck." Being able or not to look in several directions. Being "stiff necked," "sticking your neck out."

Shoulders Shouldering responsibilities or giving a shoulder to lean on, carrying burdens.

Arms   Usually about being armed or reaching out.

Hands   "Open handed"; "giving a hand out"; can or can't "handle it"; giving, receiving, touch and feeling; prayer; clean, empty, open, rough right and left.

Fingers To do with dexterity. Each finger has a special meaning which varies according to our own experiences.

Back   To do with strength, support and uprightness. Backbone, turning your back, revealing your back, someone's on your back or a pain in the back, the last straw.

Legs   Support: "having a leg to stand on." "Being weak at the knees" – showing a lack of courage. Also, kneeling and supplication.

Feet   About being grounded, taking the first step, "best foot forward," "cold feet"; heels and Achilles tendons are weak spots.

The internal organs are used so often to describe situations that simply searching your own mind should immediately give you the necessary clues: "put your heart into it," "he's taking the piss," "she's gone back into the womb," are a few phrases.

It is important to realize that all fears and emotions are hidden in the images and it is these we are trying to identify when we interpret our dreams.

SEX

Surprisingly, sexual dreams can improve our sex lives. If, in your dreams you have the most amazing erotic experiences, yet your ordinary life seems dull and mechanical, it could be that you set the wrong scenario for yourself in reality. If you are keeping a record of your dreams, you can look for the patterns. Is your dream lover always the same, or do you have a variety? How does he or she compare with your real partner? What is different in the early stages with your dream lover? Do you encourage and participate or does your lover have to do all the foreplay? What turns you on and helps you reach a climax? Sometimes we would rather not look our fears and prejudices in the face and we hide from them.

These dreams are clear messages from our deep unconscious minds. Because of this we need to be aware of the images, the sex symbols, the disguises which we also use when awake. Virtually all rigid pointed objects, such as a poker, are phallic particularly if they are being inserted into an opening or crevice. Keys come into this category but usually have a more profound meaning (see Chapter 12 on Symbols). Tools bring an immediate response since we use the word anyway as a phallic symbol. Thus screwdrivers, drills, pile drivers, hammers and nails all have double meanings, as do weapons. Rifles, swords, and daggers all show that domination is in mind.

We should also look at wilting or flexible objects. Balloons that won't inflate, a limp garden hose, a drooping flower, a damp squib or even a jack-in-a-box with a broken spring.

Top: These show real power, that you are armed for all situations.

Right: We often have sex dreams when our sex lives have become uninteresting or we are in enforced celibacy.

Frequently if a woman dreams of being attacked with any straight, rigid object, the dream is sexual.

These all indicate our fears of inadequacy and can apply equally to men and women. Other powerful images are, of course, beds and bedrooms, cocks, seeds, and especially motor cars, which in dreams are images of ourselves. The fast sportscar can be in or out of control. It can also refuse to start or run out of fuel.

The female is often veiled as a hole of some sort, an entrance, a ring. Sometimes these entrances are blocked which speaks for itself. Apples, melons, cows, nuts: these words are all part of our everyday vocabulary, so the clues are there. Sex is often described as "a fire in the belly" and lovers are "old flames." Take expressions like "he turns me on/off" – we could dream of a tap that runs dry, as water is connected with the emotions.

"Jo dreams of a smoldering fire. He picks up an old-fashioned poker and starts to encourage the flames. Quickly the fire takes hold but he pokes it so violently that the coals fall out and burn him. He finds a bucket of water and dowses the flames." This dream shows that sometime in the past, Jo deliberately stirred up a sexual passion only to discover that he could not handle it and because burns scar, he is still carrying the guilt. Dowsing the fire shows that he can be in control.

Rabbits, snakes, bulls, wolves and unicorns are frequently sexual symbols. Rabbits because they are so fertile, snakes because of their resemblance to spermatozoa, bulls for their virility, and unicorns for their horns. Of course, we are all familiar with the reputation of the wolf.

"I am with my boyfriend in a holiday cottage that is losing its walls. Suddenly a magnificent unicorn appears. Its horn curves downwards. Suddenly he charges the house, breathing rage. My boyfriend runs, while I kneel before the unicorn. It is sunset." You are in a temporary refuge which is falling apart. The unicorn represents your sexual needs which, when it charges even frightens your boyfriend, whereas you submit to him. The sunset shows the relationship is at an end.

"Sheep are being attacked by a wolf and the farmer sends hounds to kill it. The wolf crawls near me on a ledge, its skin flayed off. Then I am a hound. Then I am human again. The ledge is precarious and made of novels and some skirts. I know I am going to fall." Someone around you has earned the wolf reputation and is being harassed by colleagues. You join them and become an accessory to his downfall. Because you are not entirely innocent, you find yourself in a precarious position and the feeling that you will fall shows that you will have to confess. The narrow ledge shows the danger of a life based on romantic novels and a vicarious sex life, represented by the skirts.

In the dream state it is perfectly normal for men to have erections and women to become moist as erotic images titillate our senses. Dreams are far more exciting than porn or blue films because we are actually taking part. Lots of dreamers find this desperately embarrassing, but this is just the dream mind showing us that we're not impotent or frigid. The problem is, in everyday life, that our partners simply don't turn us on. So by reliving our dream fantasies when making love, we can make our bodies wake up, promoting unexpected and pleasurable responses from our partners.

We can also seed or incubate our dreams to enjoy our sexual fantasies. An exciting idea is to have a dream lover. This will stimulate your sexual energy and greatly enhance your love life. Just before sleeping create in your mind the most ideal place for lovemaking. Now create your most wonderful sexual partner with whom to enjoy an ecstatic night of love. As you fall asleep your dreams will take over these images and you will have the most exquisite and magical experiences. If such a dream should become lucid, imagine the possibilities.

It often takes some practice and, initially, you may find yourself with a less than perfect lover, but just persevere and soon things will improve. If you are feeling sex-starved or are in enforced celibacy, dream lovers bring untold bliss. Also, there are times in a good relationship when we feel the need for a bit of variety, and by taking a dream lover we don't threaten our partners. Go ahead and have fun.

Pregnancy and birth can be related to sex and sexual needs, but generally any form of gestation or its consequences is related to creativeness. However, if there is an underlying fear of the consequences of sexual behavior, then dreams of painful birthing, damaged or premature babies, sickness in pregnancy, or losing one's figure can all indicate this fear and explain frigidity or impotence. Dreaming of contraceptives is usually a strong warning to take care. It need not necessarily have sexual connotations, being applica-

Marilyn Monroe became every man's dream lover.

ble to any form of protection. Abortions are about loss and also miscarriages of justice.

Sexual diversions or perversions in dreams should not be feared. It is possible for the most normal of us to wonder about such things at times. Again, in the dream state, we do no one any harm, but we do have the opportunity to explore why we need such dreams. Are we distorting something that should be pleasurable into something sadistic or masochistic? Or are we, in fact, hiding from that part of our nature?

Rape demonstrates a personal invasion of some sort or something being forced on us. It is about taking advantage of weaknesses or taking by force, obliging a person to act against their will. It should always be examined from both points of view, since frequently we only see it from the feminine side. Sometimes, symbolically raping a person's deep held views has a validity of its own.

Taking off our clothes show a desire to change our image but can also indicate a sexual connection.

"My brother is watching me undress and I am ignoring him. Suddenly he grabs me and tries to kiss me. I struggle but know I can't get away. I feel disgusted at what he is trying to do to me." Being watched undressing shows that you feel exposed and rape indicates that unwanted and unpleasant things are being forced on you. It is time for you to start taking charge of your life.

NUDITY

Dreams of nudity are extremely common because they are to do with vulnerability. They occur when we find ourselves in states where we fall short of our goals or standards that others set for us and are found out, or think we are. The dream mind emphasizes our exposure. Nudity can also indicate naivety, a juvenile approach, a lack of preparation and being caught unaware. Also in this category are dreams of being caught with our pants down, or our zip unfastened, or sitting on the lavatory when the door bursts open or the walls fall down.

Usually being naked matters, and often in our dreams everyone is aware of our condition. This shows that in our waking lives we are truly making fools of ourselves even though we may not be aware of this. Sometimes, however, no one seems to notice. This indicates that our fears are our own unfounded projections of what others are thinking, which is generally very far from the truth, so there is really nothing to worry about. On other occasions we are nude, people are looking and we simply don't care. This shows that we have shed outmoded restrictions or attitudes.

Another aspect is seeing others naked, which shows that we can penetrate behind their facades. Their various reactions in the dream show how aware they are. If they are unaware of being naked, and are

being flattered and admired, then, unwittingly, they are fools. Bear in mind that this could also be an aspect of ourselves.

In the main, clothing represents our outside image. How many hours and how much money do we spend working on how we look? Consider how we dress for different occasions and situations. There are, of course, times when being naked feels really good, unencumbered and relaxing.

DEATH, KILLING AND BURIALS

At the other end of the scale is death and dying. These dreams can be precognitive and there are instances where people have dreamed of their own deaths, but this is very rare. The general view here is that such an intuition is a form of preparation for the event. It

Left: Being caught naked in public shows considerable vulnerability.

Below: Dreams of death rarely have anything to do with real death but are about a need to bring something to an end.

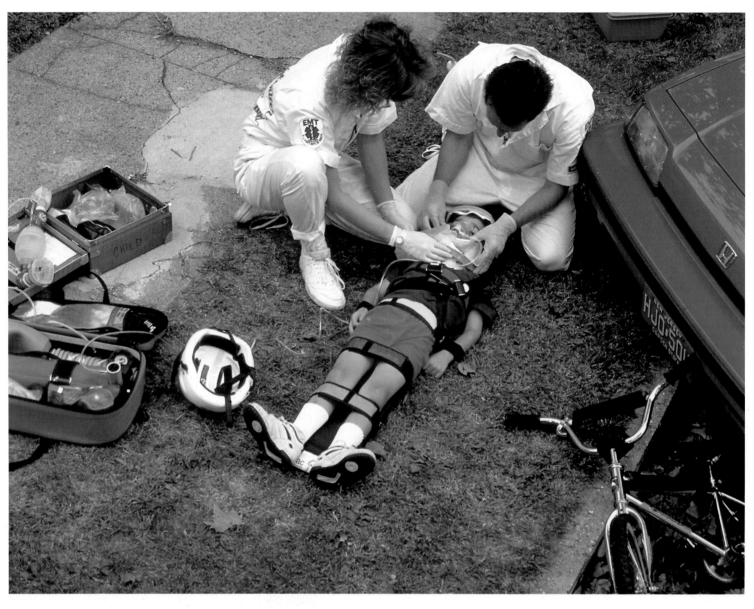

enables the dreamer to come to terms with the tragedy, to be strong and help others through the crisis. The more common meaning is that of the end of something, something that has run its course, is ready to die and be buried, or eliminated. It can apply to people, situations, habits or strong beliefs.

It can manifest itself in a number of ways. Either we see someone dead, or witness our own death, or we are killing or being killed, or are at a funeral, either ours or someone else's, or in graveyards. In each case the message is the same. It is a time of release and new beginnings. It can mean that we are wishing someone dead or we would like to kill them off, bury them and get them out of our sight, so when considering the meaning of death dreams, it is

Above: Accidents in dreams as usually warnings about our own actions and have little to do with real accidents.

Left: Dreaming of a sacrificial death shows that you need to ask yourself if the sacrifice is necessary.

Right: Sometimes it can mean that we are wishing someone dead and buried. It is important to decide if the victim is ourself.

important to decide whether the victims are ourselves or those around us in disguise.

Ritual sacrifice or torture can be a clear mirror of our waking life. Frequently we are depressed and unhappy and are unable to put a finger on why. Such dreams help us to recognize the situation and point a finger at our tormentors.

Chapter Twelve

SYMBOLS

Many people are perplexed about symbols, feeling that they have a strange esoteric meaning and wishing that they could understand them. The first thing to realize is that they are a form of shorthand to which we respond emotionally, from the very superficial to the extremely deep psychic levels. They are pictures, hieroglyphics, codes, or signs, which show one thing, but are actually saying something else, having another meaning from the obvious.

Some of them are universal and will speak to us without our conscious co-operation. Others are personal to us, our own private language or secret code. For example a pet nickname between friends; a photo of a loved one speaks directly only to the lover; a cryptic remark which recalls an incident only to the participants; a perfume or change of light which always evokes a special moment. Symbols can be geometric or abstract, a picture or an object. They are really energies to which a form is given in order to understand it. Taking the abstract, apart from the dot, most of these symbols emanate from three main geometric forms or the combination of these forms or parts thereof: the circle, the

Left: Abstract shapes that have a deeper meaning have been used by man since the beginnings of time.

Right: The geometric shapes that have the most profound influence on our unconscious minds.

vertical line, the horizontal line. These were based on the most important features of early man's natural surroundings, namely the sun, the tree and the horizon respectively.

The dot is a simple mark without elaborate form covering the minutest of areas. It represents a beginning, a seed, a desire before it becomes a thought and takes a form. It is the singular, the one, the indivisible, absolute being, the center from which all emerges and to which all returns. It can also be the navel, the unborn life force. It also represents the junction of two intersecting lines, the axis, the fulcrum. or the tip of something. However, on the written page it represents an end, the completion of a thought and, in some cases, absolute finality. When it is placed within the circle it represents the Zodiacal sun with all its male, solar and power connotations.

The spiral emanates from the dot. It is as though the dot has gone into motion and the energy spins out from it. It is one of the most ancient of symbols, discovered in the symbols of civilizations the world over. It represents the energy source, the vortex, evolution, or dragon power. It is also connected with the maze or labyrinth where the soul searches for the central source.

From the dot and the spiral, we expand into the circle, the universal symbol of the spirit. It is the zero, the all, the. nothing, the void. It has no beginning and no end. It is totality, and timelessness but is also

cyclic and repetitive, signaling endless movement. It is perfection, the same from all directions. It is the circle of spirit. When it contains the dot, it is the symbol for the sun and all sun gods, depicting cyclic completion. The space within the circle can represent enlightenment – the value of the empty space within.

It also represents the wheel of life and reincarnation – birth and rebirth. As a wheel it moves in time and space in an eternal progression. It can be the wheel of fate, of time, of karma. Or it can be a mandala drawing one in and out of its center. In its wheel aspect it manifests as the Round Table and the Zodiac. Another of its common connotations

The rod or staff which can be used as a form of support or in self defense.

ing, turning relentlessly, waiting for no man. Freeing oneself from the wheel is one of the aims of the seeker. Another aspect is to free oneself from the velocity of the rim and move to the stillness of the center.

Other wheels are the Zodiac, with all its complicated hidden meanings; its constant motion of the planets through the heavens influences the cyclic patterns of the soul on earth. In the same category is the Arthurian Round Table – its knights representing different archetypal aspects of the psyche.

Twin circles represent the male and female aspects. They also form the figure 8 which has many meanings from the final stage of the initiate, to the number of the musical octave, to the eight limbs of Yoga, to mention just a few. Turned on its side and elongated it becomes the lemniscate, the sign of infinity. Although common in mathematical symbology it can also be found above the head of the Magician in the Tarot pack, indicating that he can be in touch with all knowledge.

The half-circle is related to the mind, the soul, and the moon with its phases of waxing and waning. Facing to the left is waxing, expansion, and growth; to the right is waning, retreating, dying; above facing the ground is protective, enveloping, eliminating; below facing upwards is receptive, containing, a source of nourishment. In its latter position it is also a symbol for water. It is also connected with the rainbow commonly thought to be the bridge between heaven and earth, this world and the next. It is a symbol of hope, a creation of fire and water, sun and rain.

The straight line across the center of a circle represents division: two hemispheres, two polarities, consciousness and unconsciousness, heaven and earth, logical left brain/intuitive right brain. The curve or S shape within a circle indicates perfect balance of the two main energies of the universe as in the yin-yang symbol. This sign contains the essence of the one within the other

is that of the disk or shield equating with earth, money and protection. In heraldry it is known as a roundel, the gold version, often found in the crests of banks, being a bezant. Circles form an enclosure, a place of protection and safety, as is seen in the earth circles, camp circles, or wigwams. It can be considered as a containment of the spiritual world, as in stone circles or, round churches.

When a circle appears with wings it is the spirit joined by the element air. It is the symbol of the heavenly

messenger, disseminating heavenly knowledge. Although it is manifestly male in its relationship to the sun, the circle also has female connections as the cup and the pool, the space within and the Cosmic Egg. From the circle we get the wheel, which appears in many different patterns with and without spokes. The most familiar form is the wheel of life or wheel of fortune, indicating cyclic existence, birth and re-birth. It is also related to time, fate and karma. It is considered to be enslav-

Above: The Cosmic Egg, a manifestation of the circle, the source of all life forms.

Right: Many of the basic shapes are used in heraldry, the purpose of which was to recognize friends and foes in battle.

indicating that for perfection both must blend and be equal.

From the dot or the seed, emerges the root and the shoot, making the next natural mark, a vertical line. In nearly all cultures, this represents the male/positive/active principle or spirit, which by virtue of its vertical position could either rise or descend. Its shape joins two points, it creates a route between the above and the below; from the zero of infinity to the two of duality. It brings matter into manifestation. It also represents the rod, the staff or the wand. The staff is the help mate, a support, a form of defense and also of attack. It can be an instrument of

Again the use of a universal language to convey a message. Like the Tarot these have double meanings.

pain as a whip, a goad or an arrow, or a penetrator as a needle or a drill. As a rod it can be a spindle or axis. It can be used for measuring and as a flute, to make music. In its phallic sense it represents fertilization both actual and spiritual. In Runic it is the symbol of ice, of a period of waiting, holding and renewal. As a wand – the pointed finger – it means concentrated power and energy rather like a channeled laser beam. It is also the symbol for the number one, and the basis of our present Roman letters, as well as Ogham and Runic scripts.

In the horizontal line there is the female/negative/receptive principle or matter. It is about settling down and finding a level horizon, or surface. It is the waiting principle rely-ing on instincts and intuition. It is also the horizontal axis where the high changes places with the low. Or it can be seen as a bridge, like the vertical, a linking of two points. As a horizon, it offers limitations, but also hidden possibilities, the "something" beyond conscious vision. As a surface it offers protection as a roof, or stability and support, as in chairs and tables, or simply the solid earth. However, one must remember its elusive darker side, the level waters of instability, reflections, and unseen depths, into which one can fall. It is also the womb, the place of fertiliza-tion, the beginning of all things.

Parallel lines represent duality and separation, the important fea-ture being that they never meet. They are the division of the one into the two, to the area of opposites and polarities. They can also indicate balance and equality – the scales of justice.

The combination of three straight lines is related to the Trinity, the three fold nature of the universe: heaven, earth and man; body, soul and spirit; god, man, and woman; father, son, and holy ghost; creator, preserver, and destroyer; desire, thought, and form. In their vertical position they create the trident, from which is derived the fleur-de-lys. It is a symbol of power and status as is evidenced as the weapon of Poseidon or King Neptune. It is also the trident of Shiva symbolizing his threefold character. We also know it as the sign of the Devil. The fleur-de-lys is the emblem of the kings of

France and also of Britain's Prince of Wales.

Three lines joined together become a triangle, and the equilateral triangle is most common. The upward pointing shape is the fire symbol (truncated it is air) related to the male and the sun. It is the asking, demanding aspect and is frequently used in meditation to ask questions of the sub-conscious or the higher self. The inverted triangle is water (truncated it is earth) the female, lunar aspect. It is receptive, the cave, the womb, the secret source. In meditation it is used to receive answers.

Stars are common symbols, usually seen with five, six, seven, nine and twelve points. The five-pointed star, the pentagram is the symbol of man: this is clear in Leonardo's drawing of a naked man within the star. When it is pointing upwards it is the symbol of good, related to the spirit, and to creation. It is frequently used as a symbol of protection and

Right: Stars have fascinated mankind for many centuries with many legends woven around them.

Below: The fleur-de-lys, symbol of the French court and also the personal symbol of the Prince of Wales.

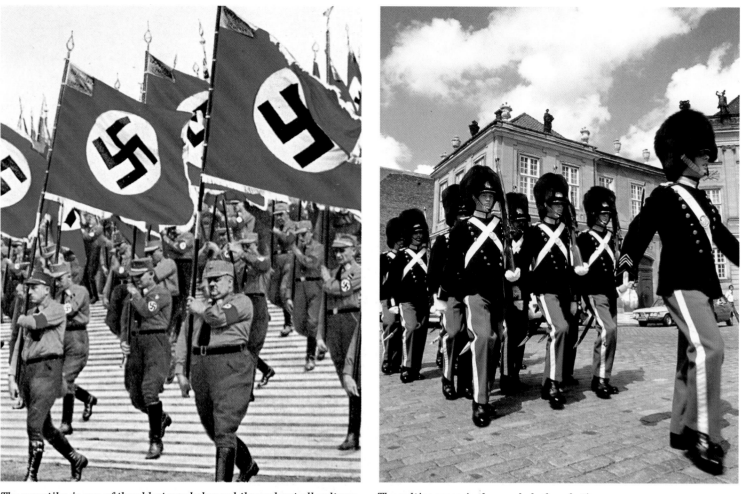

The swastika is one of the oldest symbols used throughout all cultures.   *The saltire cross is the symbol of perfection.*

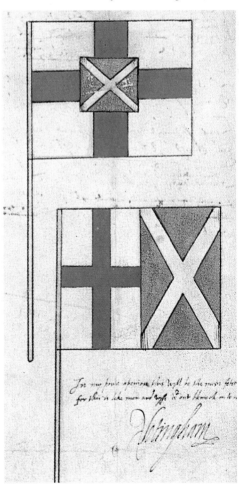

Many national flags are composed of these geometric elements.

is also important in banishing rituals. It is used extensively in magic and has a number of different meanings according to how it is drawn, mainly related to the elements. When it is inverted, it is said to represent evil and black magic.

The six-pointed star, the star of David or hexagram, represents a combination of fire and water – active into passive, positive into negative to obtain perfect balance. It is also the union of the higher and lower self for which each soul is striving. Again, it is useful as a protection. In Yogic thinking it relates to the heart center and the powers of air.

Four straight lines usually manifest as a square, the symbol of earth. The threefold plus the fourth equals totality, order, limitation. From the circular tents and encampments of the nomadic peoples we move to the static square houses of the agrarian peoples. It represents solidity, dependability, earthiness and the security of the balanced base. It is the foundation that supports the structure. It brings us once more back to all the connections of the number four – the four seasons, the four quarters of the moon, the four archangels, the four times of day, the four evangelists, and the four elements to mention a few. In each instance, it is the earthly aspect that relates to the square. When turned on its side it becomes a diamond or lozenge. It represents the feminine principle, the yoni. It is also the symbol for time. It is also connected with money or the suit of diamonds/disks in playing cards.

The pyramid is the three-dimensional conjunction of the dot, the triangle and the square. It is the joining of fire and earth and is a symbol of great antiquity. Often known as the sacred mountain, with the steps upwards being the planes of consciousness, it is also considered to be a place of initiation and a route to altered states of consciousness. It is well documented that placing articles under pyramid shapes enhances them. The joining of the vertical with the horizontal represents the descent of spirit into matter, the act of fertilization which creates life on all levels. Other schools of thought see it as the spine (spirit) penetrating the body (matter); or the vertical as the Pole Star bisecting the rising Sun (horizontal).

The cross is the universal symbol of man, indicating his ability to extend in all directions. It is the union of opposites, of the androgynous nature of the perfected man. It is the symbol of the combination of the four. It has the four cardinal points, the four elements, the four rivers of paradise, in fact, everything that is related to four.

The equidistant cross in the circle is also an ancient symbol. It is the cross of man in the wheel of change, of earth within spirit. The four arms represent the elements contained within the wisdom of the spirit. It is good fortune, but also change. It is the solar energy, the part of fortune and the universal symbol of protection, especially for meditation. It is well known as the Celtic Cross or the Lodge Cross, and in the Runes it is the solar wheel, representing spiritual power, law and order, contained religious force.

The equidistant cross with a circle at the center represents the chakra of the Hindu teachings. It also represents the essence, the unity of the four elements. With a rose at the center, it is harmony but also secrecy, this being the meaning of the rose. It is also the combination of the cross and the wheel showing divinity combined with sacrifice.

The elongated vertical line is said to signify the deeper descent into matter to initiate transformation, although some say that it is because Catholicism concentrated its teachings on the mind rather than the heart which is the center of a normal cross. It is the symbol of Christianity

The equidistant cross within the circle is one of the greatest symbols of protection.

and of the love of Christ. Originally crucifixion was a punishment for the criminal, but now it signifies the ultimate martyrdom, the giving of all, even life itself to achieve the perfection of God. Thus it represents sacrifice, suffering, redemption and, for some cultures, great iniquity. It should be noted that most churches are built in this shape.

The swastika is probably one of the oldest symbols and is found throughout virtually all world cultures, from China and Japan, through Hinduism, and Islam, to Northern Europe. Its main meaning seems to be related to motion. It is sometimes described as a circle with sections removed from the quarters which gives a sense of rotation. It has two forms, the masculine which revolves clockwise, and the feminine revolving anticlockwise, which signify its solar and lunar aspects. In its solar or masculine form it signifies creative force, motion, whirling

The sword represents the spirit, the energizing principle and protection.

known as the key of life, the entrance to all wisdom and mystery. It combines the eternal, cyclic perfection of the circle spiritually penetrating the horizontal of matter, enjoining the source of all wisdom with the mundane. It is the union of male and female. It is the symbol of Isis both in role as High Priestess and eternal Mother. It can also signify the sun rising and sinking over the horizon, cyclic completion and regeneration. It is also an alternative shape for many churches and cathedrals rather than the crucifix.

The caduceus is the combination of the vertical line, the two spirals and the winged disk. The correct format shows the spirals crossing four times before uniting at the top. It is the symbol of Mercury, the messenger of the gods, of Thoth, the healer and keeper of wisdom, of medicine indicating the four humors and healing. The vertical line of spirit descends into matter represented by the crossing of the spirals. The spirals also represent the duality, the two forces of positive, yang (right hand path) and negative yin, (left hand path). According to Yogic tradition, when the two pathways are clear and the energies are flowing freely through the cleared chakras, the sleeping serpent – the kundalini – awakens and shoots up the spine, the central pillar, into the head bringing enlightenment. The winged disk represents the circle of the spirit communicated.

Numbers can be explored in relation to their shape or as part of numerology, a huge subject in its own right. Arabic numerals, used in

chaos from a creative center, good fortune and perfection. Its lunar/feminine form is the female generative power, the divine force and very occasionally submission (meaning learning through allowing). One can see why it was used by the Nazis because of its universality and perfection. In the Runic tradition it is solar power transmutation and magical power under will. Sounding and chanting the runes brings much power and control.

The saltire cross is the symbol of perfection. It is the cross of both St. Andrew of Scotland and St. Patrick of Ireland. It is also the sign for the number ten which is the natural expression of totality, of the completion of cycles, of starting again. It sometimes signifies suffering and martyrdom. In Runic it means a partnership or gift. There is also another Runic symbol, Naudhiz, the need fire, combining the vertical with the diagonal meaning. Basically it is protection, but in the sense of distress and deliverance from distress – a learning through hardship.

The ankh is the cross surmounted by the circle. This is commonly

Below: Dream shapes come in many forms, several have ancient symbolism.

123456789

13
666
999

the West, closely resemble the symbols above of triangles, squares and stars. Before we start looking for special esoteric or obscure meanings relating to numbers in dreams, we should explore special dates, house and telephone numbers, formulae, appointments, times of the day, in fact anything which alludes to numbers.

Zero, like the circle, represents the infinite, the void, the all embracing and the emptiness.

Number one is the monad, the beginnings, the source. It is also the most important, the first, indivisible unity with the Godhead, growth without change of form. It is also phallic and connected with the masculine. It can be seen as isolation, oddness and eccentricity.

Number two represents duality and division, polarity and partner-

Above and right: Out of number comes form.

ships. It is the number of manifestation and deals with opposites and balance. It shows a coming together, partnerships or a splitting apart, the two halves of something. Also, it is about reflections and equality.

Number three is the Trinity, the third force that results from putting the two together. It is the desire, thought and action which gives rise to form. It gives added strength forming a base as in a tripod. It is also worth considering that two is company and three is a crowd.

Number four usually represents the physical and the earth principles. Solidity, materialism and the mundane. There are endless associations with the number four: four seasons, four quarters, four winds, four ele-

Abstract shapes that have a deeper meaning used by man since the beginnings of time.

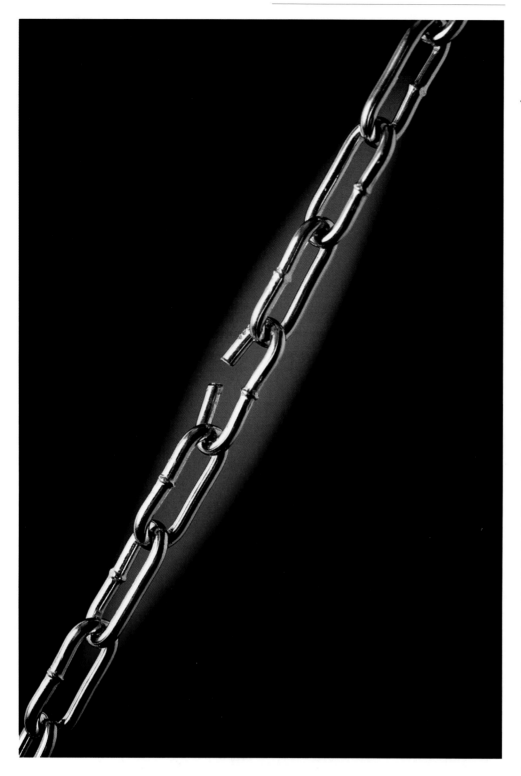

Left: The secret of numbers is their sequence. One missing causes a break in the chain.

Right: Out of numbers comes architectural form.

to time and rhythm which appears over and over again – seven ages of man, seven days of the week, seven colors in the spectrum, seven notes to the scale.

Number eight is connected with material wealth, money, balance and infinity. It is the lemniscate, the abbreviated sign for infinity. It is the cube and, therefore, connected with salt which crystallizes in cubes. It is also the corner stone. It represents the eight arms of wisdom, the eight fold path to true fulfillment, the sanctification of the temple in eight days.

Number nine is the final single digit number and, therefore, is to do with endings or completions. Nine was known as the Concord because it unites and knits together all other numbers.

Number ten is the decimal counting number, and is about new beginnings and totality. In a way it is the number one amplified. It contains every other number within itself. There are many 10s to be found in the ancient scriptures and the mystical system of the Kabbala has ten sephiroth.

Number eleven is often considered to be the number of power, mastery and enlightenment. It is about perfection running parallel. It is a higher expression of numbers one and two.

Number twelve is about cycles and is a composite of two, three, four and six and a higher expression of three. Although cyclic it is also known as the number of space. Like seven, it is found everywhere – twelve months, twelve hours, twelve disciples, twelve tribes, twelve titans, and twelve labors of Hercules to name a few.

Number thirteen is only unlucky if given this interpretation, which stems from the Last Supper when 13 sat down at table. In reality it is a higher expression of the four and is

ments, four gospels. It is about coming together in groups and a certain amount of dependency.

Number five is known as the number of mankind and the five senses, the five appendages to the body, five fingers and toes. It is the number of striving and summons – the fifth trumpet. We are now in the fifth root race.

Number six is the number of balance and harmony. It is known as the number of creation being a com-

posite of the three. The quartz crystal has six sides and is important to this Age. It was the sacred number of the Druids. 666, of course, is the number of the beast from the book of Revelation. The beast can be associated with Satan, but also with the untapped energies on a soul level, the sleeping serpent.

Number seven has always held a special place in our culture being connected with the seven days of creation. It is very cyclic and related

Crowns, hats and headdresses are symbols of authority.

often expressed as 12 + 1 being the number of space and its leader. It is about change and transition, death and re-birth.

Most dreams are in color but generally we are not particularly aware of this unless some aspect is brought to our attention. Colors create atmospheres and can have an overall livening or muting effect, so if there is a dominance of red, for example, there are two possibilities. Either we are lacking in energy and stimulation or we have too much. This can apply equally to our surroundings or

Right: The chequered flag, the emotive combination of black and white.

The seven colors of the spectrum form a rainbow.

clothing, and, the dream is emphasizing our need to take in the significance.

If the colors in your dream are particularly vivid and dramatic then it could be a precognitive dream, although this is not a foolproof guarantee (see Chapter 4). Dreaming in black and white is fairly common and often has no significance. Sometimes, though, it can mean that your life has become colorless or that the dream is about the past.

If when you dress in the morning you feel a certain color does absolutely nothing for you and you look flat and dull, replace it immediately with a color which makes you glow. As mentioned in Chapter 3, we all have an aura which is multicolored and what we wear and how we feel definitely tones in with it. Your dreams can show you that, through bad use of color, you are deflating yourself.

The seven colors of the spectrum, plus black and white, all have marked significance and research has shown that they can strongly influence how we react. There are many secondary and tertiary colors which lie in between the major ones and these can be studied in depth elsewhere. The meanings for the major ten are fairly standard.

Red is the basic color and is to do with raw energy. This can be interpreted as strength to carry out manual tasks, vitality, will power, stimulation and motivation. On the other hand, it also symbolizes anger, frustration, revenge, impatience or embarrassment. People who wear red tend to be very physical or manual expressing themselves through their bodies, and expressions such as "red rag to a bull," " I saw red," or "a scarlet woman" show this.

Orange is the color of groups where the raw energy is blended and used for joint enterprises. It is about joining, expansion, sexuality, friendliness and sociability, fruitfulness and ripeness. It used to be the color worn by condemned criminals and is now the color of the robes of the Buddhist orders. Orange people are very social or involved in the community. Orange-tawny was a color worn by money lenders; orange blossom is a symbol of fruitfulness for brides; "Orangemen" are Irish Protestants, once the supporters of William of Orange.

Yellow, strangely, relates to intellect, self-discipline, mental discrimination and detachment, and the converse sides are excessive criticism, cynicism and fear, also jealousy and adultery. Yellow is often equated with gold and those in gold are often expressing their achievements. Expressions such as "yellow belly," or having a "yellow streak," emphasize the fearful qualities, and the French used to daub yellow on the doors of traitors. Judas, the disciple who betrayed Jesus is often portrayed in yellow.

Green is to do with love and harmony, generosity and nurture. It can be young, fresh and immature. It is thought to be the color of healing and growth. Conversely it represents inexperience and jealousy and can be muting and depressing. Expressions are "looking green round the gills," "going green with envy," and possessing "green thumbs." In some places, such as Scotland, it is deemed to be unlucky to wear green because it was worn at the Battle of Flodden where the Scots were decimated by the English in the fifteenth century. It is much more common nowadays, but could be explained as the color of blending or camouflage.

Blue is the color of peace, but also of authority and teaching. Patience, nurture, forgiveness and understanding are also attributes. Conversely it can be thought cold, isolated, detached, passive, depressed. It is frequently connected with communication and vocal expression. This is the standard color for uniforms which represent conforming or being made to conform. Expressions which influence our thinking are "being a true blue," "feeling blue," or being "a blue stocking."

Indigo is related to intuition and the ability to foresee or divine. It represents beauty and asceticism. It is useful for healing eye problems. Its opposite is pure logic or obtuseness. This is really the color of twilight and early dawn, times of transition when one's awareness leads to heightened perception.

Violet is about inspiration, meditation, spiritual consciousness, religion. In its pinker tones it indicates love and compassion. Its opposite features are an inability to live in the present, spaced out, day-dreaming, isolation. In its darker tones it is worn by royalty and the clergy, but is becoming more and more popular in all its shades as a spiritual color.

Magenta indicates a quality of organization, the ability to take one's

Candles signify the light of the world. We can also burn them at both ends.

self in hand and of altruism. It is about administration and running large organizations. The opposite is complete chaos and incompetence. It is really the spiritual side of red, thus a blending of the material with the higher mind.

White is a combination of all the colors of the spectrum. It signifies purity, innocence, unsullied things, virginity, simplicity and candor. Alternatively, it can be blinding or dazzling preventing us from seeing clearly. It is commonly worn as a symbol of innocence/purity by brides, noviciates, babies and also to offset the strength of other colors. Many phrases emphasize the purity aspect, such as "white as snow."

Black is really no color. It is connected with mourning, death and funerals in the Western world. It is the color associated with night, with fear and the mysterious, but also with hatred and vindictiveness, gloom and depression. It can also be a shade of great comfort and retreat, to be snug in the dark. It is generally worn to conform – the uniform, the dark suit, the little black dress. Alternatively, it can evoke strong passions and fears in the sensuous dress or the all covering cloak.

There are a number of items and symbols that represent something else or have a clear dual meaning. When they appear in dreams, we should rarely take them at their face value.

Altars are invariably places of sacrifice even though their more acceptable meaning is that of worship or protection. Columns and pillars are doorways, ways through to changed consciousness. When we cross the threshold our perceptions are transformed.

The importance of candles affects us all. Their use in churches firstly as the eternal light and secondly as a sign of our devotion is well known. The flame of enlightenment is what we are all trying to achieve to lighten our darkness. The image is often used to signify the "light of the world." They also symbolize the melting down of rigid beliefs and the

opportunity, through fire, to transform. They are also about being prepared. We find them lighting our way through times past, before electricity, showing that we need to throw light on something. The place they are lighting is important. Their dangers in the form of dripping wax and naked flames should also be considered. Their other meaning is that of romance, our flaming hearts and candlelit dinners.

Crowns and headdresses are symbols of power. They set a person apart and, unless hereditary, have to be won or earned. Thus in dreams they can show where your aspirations lie, that you can be crowned with success, or that you have not yet recognized your achievements. The interesting point about crowns is that they touch the area of the third eye (intuition) and do not cover the crown of the head, leaving this open for linking with higher levels of consciousness. Also, most headgear is circular, (see the circle above). The crowns of Egypt were apparently specifically designed to channel spiritual energies. These can be seen today in the mitres of the upper clergy.

Hats, on the other hand, actually cover the crown and protect the individual from the weather, sporting activities or an excess of spiritual thinking and higher level consciousness. Think of the fact that women are expected to keep their heads covered in many different circumstances. Jewish men wear skull caps as do Roman Catholic prelates. Hats can also be forms of identification. They either set a person apart or show his allegiances. If only one person present is wearing a hat, it is impossible not to notice. Equally, when everyone wears identical hats, they lose their identity or have to have distinguishing marks. So why are you wearing your dream hat? Is it to channel higher consciousness, to stand out in a crowd, to protect yourself or to hide yourself?

The Holy Grail or the Cauldron, is one of the most powerful cup symbols of all time. Heroes go on the

Quest to retrieve it, to reach illumination and the highest states of wisdom. Many legends tell of its mystical and spiritual overtones. Always look and listen for the message as it relates to your personal quest. They are connected with water and the emotions. On more mundane levels, they are about the receptive side of ourselves. We use them to quench our thirst, or we can look deep into their contents and divine messages like the seeresses of the past. The Cup can also represent ourselves. Throwaway cups, plain white utility cups, ordinary tea cups, and mugs are fairly self-explanatory. Decorated tea cups indicate an appreciation of yourself. Trophies represent prizes, a need to be won or hard to get. Chalices can set you apart, especially those encrusted with jewels, which show a strong ego. This need not necessarily be derogatory, but one needs to be sure there is not an inflated opinion that is not justified. They can also be the source of wisdom in the same way as the cauldron, or even a religious leaning. Metal cups depend on the metal: iron, business-like and down to earth; steel, hard-nosed and tough; silver, soft with quality; gold, of great value, but also greed. Wooden cups show a self-made person or one who fashions with care and attention. It is important to ascertain whether the cups are cracked or chipped, dirty or tarnished. This again is fairly self-explanatory. It shows how you see yourself.

The eye was discussed under parts of the body. However, when seen independently of the body, it is the all-seeing eye of the cosmic source, the collective unconscious or our own deep unconscious minds. If in a dream, we have the chance to walk through the eye, it is usually quite revelationary and sometimes mystical.

The feather appears in dreams surprisingly often. It can indicate wisdom or cowardice. Also it shows achievement and great deeds, as in the North American headdresses.

Trees, the oldest living things to be found on the planet.

They can also symbolize the ability to fly. Ruffled feathers, however, show unease or insults, while flying feathers indicate anger, rows, and fighting. If they come in the form of down, comfort and warmth are probably the meanings.

Flags are one of the most powerful symbols representing patriotism. In

The rose is the symbol of love and romance but also of secrecy.

action is in the present.

The mirror is quite an important symbol. Initially, it shows us the true image of ourselves and can throw up our narcissistic tendencies. Alternatively, we can use it as a shield from any negativity directed at us. Its reflection returns to its source as in the legend of Perseus who destroyed the Gorgon by showing her her own image mirrored in his shield.

Names in dreams are generally puns and sometimes appear as anagrams. We have to dig very deeply into our psyches to find their source. They should not be glossed over.

Rings can represent the abstract circle (see above) or can be finger rings. The latter indicate a joining together, partnerships, marriages. They are about a long-term commitment. Alternatively, they can show bondage and entrapment. If they are broken, it means that the relationship is in jeopardy.

Royalty comes in a similar context to the national flag in that it represents the establishment, the whole of the governing system. It is still natural to bow or curtsey to kings and queens. We expect high standards of behavior from them. When we meet them in dreams, it can show that we are being accepted by those in power over us, or that we want to be acknowledged by them and are feeling overlooked and neglected.

The rose is generally accepted as the symbol of love and romance. However, on other levels it represents secrecy, femininity, and beauty. Its thorns indicate pain and martyrdom. A rosette signifies levels of success.

The sword or wand can either be considered as a weapon or a form of defense. The sword is thought to indicate the descent of spirit into matter which then results in action. In shape it resembles the crucifix and the caduceus. Mythologically, it was used to slay the dragon which represented evil and negativity so it was a symbol of the triumph of good. It is important to remember that it is two edged. Also, it is symbol of honor and power as shown by King

itself, it is simply a piece of colored material attached to a pole. However, it catches our attention and we usually treat it with respect. We follow it in battle and in team games. We salute it. We lower it and take it with us when we leave. At half-mast it indicates a death. In the dream world, it could be showing us that we need to support our country and all it stands for. Alternatively, it could indicate that we do not respect ourselves and all that we stand for, since each one of us is his own little kingdom.

The key is a source of currently needed information. If it is a house key, does it take you into the hall, a place of transit or into the kitchen, a place of nourishment? If it is a car key, you need to make a journey, the information is somewhere else. Keys to cellars or dungeons indicate an need to explore what you are suppressing. Cupboard keys represent what is hidden away. Keys to jewel boxes mean that there is something valuable to be found. Old keys usually mean that you have been a long time becoming aware of the need to explore the locks in yourself. New ones usually show

The Holy Grail is the most powerful symbol of all time.

Arthur's sword Excalibur. The wand can be used for beating off attack or as a shield. It is also a support in the form of a staff. In its magical sense its slim shape is an extension of the finger and a focus of magical thought and energy.

Trees are the most important of symbols to the human mind. They are among the oldest and largest forms of life on this planet, up to 2,500 years old and thus, having witnessed so many millennium, are considered to be a great source of wisdom. It is also thought that their vertical axis relates to man's upright stance. Since it is believed that the root pattern resembles and balances the branches, the tree can represent a linkage through its trunk of heaven and earth. The energy from the earth flows upwards and the knowledge from heaven down – as above, so below. They are often called the psychic protectors of the landscape.

There are trees connected with all cultures, religions and forms of worship, from the Tree of Knowledge to the crucifix. Sometimes their form is disguised as in the maypole, the menorah, the totem pole, the burning bush, the clinging vine, the beanstalk, the world tree, Yggdrasill, Christmas trees, or mistletoe. All these forms are about linking the spiritual with the mundane.

Certain trees such as the beech, oak or rowan are associated with sacred groves. These were places of worship in times past used on the major cycles of the year for linking with spiritual sources. They were circles of trees, usually of a single variety, often marked on the four quarters by another variety such as pines. Pines were also signal trees, linking sacred spots over long distances. Some of these groves can still be found today, since the original trees have seeded themselves and been nurtured by the "men of the trees" who also still exist.

When trees appear significantly in your dreams and demand your attention, consider firstly if they are only one variety, a mixture or in a grove. A wood is about the people around you at present. If the trees are tall and well spaced, this indicates well-balanced relationships. If they are distant, then you are probably not relating very well at present. If they encroach, snatch at you or get in your way, this is fairly self-explanatory. Are you growing freely or being overshadowed or strangled? Are you wilting or strong? The state of the leaves is also relevant. What season of the year is it? Sometimes trees are verdant on one side and dying on the other. Left is your logical side and right your intuitional, so bear this in mind.

In conclusion, it seems appropriate to quote from the *Upanishads*.

"Abandoning his body by the gate of dreams, the Spirit beholds in awaking his sense sleeping . . . And in the region of dreams, wandering above and below, the spirit makes for himself innumerable subtle creations. Sometimes he seems to rejoice in the love of fairy beauties, sometimes he laughs or beholds awe-inspiring terrible visions.

People see his field of pleasures; but he can never be seen."

PICTURE CREDITS
The author and publisher would like to thank Design 23 and Helen Jarvis, the indexer. We are grateful to the following individuals and institutions for permission to use the photographs on the pages noted below.

Author's Collection, pages 43 (top), 85, 88, 96 (below left)

Bettmann Archive, pages: 4 (top), 6, 7, 8, 9, 11, 12, 13, 14 (both), 16, 17, 19, 20, 21, 30, 34, 35, 53, 54 (both), 55, 56 (both), 59 (both), 61, 62, 66, 67, 70, 95, 96 (top), 102, 103, 107, 114 (both), 115, 142, 150

Bettmann/Reuters, pages: 36, 42, 43 (bottom), 44 (both)

BPL, pages: 38, 43 (top), 44 (below), 46, 51, 57, 58, 70 (both), 74, 86-87, 96 (both), 109 (bottom), 113 (bottom), 119 (bottom), 120 (bottom two), 127, 132, 134, 138, 141 (both), 143 (both), 144 (bottom), 145, 148 (left), 149, 153, 155, 157

British Museum, page: 96 (below right), 136 (below)

Shelia Burnett, pages: 67, 94, 128, 129, 130 (left), 137

Courtauld Institute of Art, page 2 (below)

Ffotograff © Charles Aithie, page 24

FPG International © Laurence B. Aiuppy 135 (below); © Color Box 89; © Charly Franklin 4 (bottom), 65, 68, 69, 72, 139, 143 (top); © G. French 110(below); © Rob Gage 93, 97(right); © Richard and Vi Gassman 111 (top); © Richard Gaul 136 (top) , 141 (top); © Rob Goldman 131 (below) © Peter Gridley 91; © Mark Gottlieb 48; © Michael Keller 99 (right); © Richard Laird 153; © Dick Luria 99 (below); L.O.L. Inc. 77 (right), 108 (top); © Michael

Nelson 100; © J. Neubauer 99 (left); © Diane Padys 152; © Barbara Peacock 40 (below); © Mike Peters 81; © James Porto 45, 64; © G. Randall 110 (top); © Stephanie Rausser 3; © Ken Reid 111 (below); © Ron Rovtar 158; © Galen Rowell 109 (top); © A. Scmidecker 105; © Chip Simons 87, 92, 101; © Clyde Smith 127 (right); © Andrea Sperling 37, 90; © J. E. Stevenson 102; © Jeffrey Sylvester 106 (top); © Thayer Syme 86, 112 (below); © Telegraph Colour Library: 4 (center), 32, 40 (top), 41, 46, 47, 52, 60, 73, 76-7 (all three), 84, 104, 113 (top), 116, 117, 119 (both),124 (top), 125 (top), 132, 151, 156; © Arthur Tilley 124 (below); © John Terence Turner 112 ; © J. Zimmerman 80

CHM Pictures, page 106 (below)

Hulton-Deutsch, pages: 2 (top), 10, 15 (both), 50 (both), 62, 63, 75 (both), 78, 79, 82, 83, 84-5, 86, 86-7, 98, 119 (top), 122 (bottom), 123, 126-7, 130 (right), 134-5

Irish Tourist Board, pages 118-119, 121 (top), 139, 145

Life File © Caroline Field 26 (bottom); © Nigel Sitwell 25; © Andrew Watson 27

Lowie Museum of Anthropology, University of California, Berkeley, page: 31

Photo Network, pages: 10, 22, 23,

Prediction Magazine, page: 29

154.6
F8195

117504

3 4711 00179 9172